Scott Foresman
Writing Rubrics and Anchor Papers

PEARSON

Scott Foresman

Editorial Offices: Glenview, Illinois
Parsippany, New Jersey • New York, New York
Sales Offices: Boston, Massachusetts
Duluth, Georgia • Glenview, Illinois
Coppell, Texas • Sacramento, California • Mesa, Arizona

ISBN: 0-328-14724-9

3 4 5 6 7 8 9 10 V001 12 11 10 09 08 07

Contents

Unit Rubrics

Weekly Rubrics

Support for Writing

Suggestions for Using This Book

This book is most effective when used in conjunction with the weekly and unit writing lessons in Scott Foresman's *Reading Street.* Rubrics and anchor papers can be copied and distributed or made into transparencies. Here are some ways to use the materials.

- Distribute copies of page v to students. Work through the explanations of traits with the class to develop background for discussing scores.

- Display one-by-one the four models for a given mode in order (starting with Score 1 or Score 4). Work through the commentaries that appear below the models to illustrate how each got its score.

- After students become proficient with determining scores, distribute copies of writing models from this book with the scores screened out. Work with students to arrive at scores.

- Display a model that is Score 1. Work with students to improve the model.

- Display the rubric for the type of writing you are teaching. Have students use the rubric to evaluate their own writing.

- Distribute copies of the Self-Evaluation Guide on page vi. Have students use this guide to evaluate their work.

Tips for Teaching and Evaluating Writing

- Choose one writing trait to emphasize each week. Appoint a team of students for each trait. Have them find their trait in selections they read and in their own writing and present their findings to the class.

- Read short passages from literature (for example, a tall tale) and from other content areas (for example, a science text). Point out how writer's purpose determines voice, word choice, and style.

- Remember that a writer may be more proficient in one trait than in another. To arrive at a score, evaluators must weigh proficiency in all traits.

- Tell students that when they evaluate their own writing, assigning a score of 3, 2, or even 1 does not necessarily indicate a failure. The ability to identify areas for improvement in future writing is a valuable skill.

- Encourage students to think of themselves as writers. Alert them that subjects, words, and ideas are everywhere. Suggest they keep a notebook handy to record material, such as overheard conversations, sentences from their reading, and vivid words they encounter.

- Join students as they write. Share your own writing with them and ask for their feedback on your work.

- Model constructive ways of giving feedback on writing. *(Words such as* pounce *and* swat *give me a good picture of your cat. You said her name is Boots. How did she get that name? You mentioned that she has a favorite place to sleep. Could you describe it?)*

Traits

- Focus/Ideas
- Organization/ Paragraphs
- Voice
- Word Choice
- Sentences
- Conventions

- **Focus/Ideas** refers to the main purpose for writing and the details that make the subject clear and interesting. It includes development of ideas through support and elaboration.

- **Organization/Paragraphs** refers to the overall structure that guides readers through a piece of writing. Within that structure, transitions show how ideas, sentences, and paragraphs are connected.

- **Voice** shows the writer's unique personality and establishes a connection between writer and reader. Voice, which contributes to style, should be suited to the audience and the purpose for writing.

- **Word Choice** is the use of precise, vivid words to communicate effectively and naturally. It helps create style through the use of specific nouns, lively verbs and adjectives, and accurate, well-placed modifiers.

- **Sentences** covers strong, well-built sentences that vary in length and type. Skillfully written sentences have pleasing rhythms and flow fluently.

- **Conventions** refers to mechanical correctness and includes grammar, usage, spelling, punctuation, capitalization, and paragraphing.

Self-Evaluation Guide

Name ____

Name of Writing Product _______________________________

Directions Review your final draft. Then rate yourself on a scale from 4 to 1 (4 is the highest) on each writing trait. After you fill out the chart, answer the questions.

Writing Traits	4	3	2	1
Focus/Ideas				
Organization/Paragraphs				
Voice				
Word Choice				
Sentences				
Conventions				

1. What is the best part of this piece of writing? Why do you think so?

____

____

____

____

2. Write one thing you would change about this piece of writing if you had the chance to write it again.

____

____

____

____

Rubric	6	5	4	3	2	1
Focus/Ideas	Personal narrative clearly focused; strong elaboration	Personal narrative well focused; good elaboration	Personal narrative mostly focused; some elaboration	Personal narrative with unclear focus; little elaboration	Personal narrative often off topic; weak elaboration	Personal narrative with no focus or elaboration
Organization/ Paragraphs	Clear sequence of events; excellent beginning, middle, end	Mostly clear sequence; good beginning, middle, end	Generally clear sequence; beginning, middle, end	Some events out of sequence; weak beginning or end	Confused sequence of events; lacks beginning or ending	No attempt to put events into sequence
Voice	Sincere, engaging, unique voice	Clear, engaging voice	Sincere, pleasant voice	Pleasant voice but not compelling or unique	No clear, original voice	Uninvolved or indifferent
Word Choice	Vivid descriptive words that invoke sensory response	Vivid words that describe subject; some appeal to senses	Some vivid sensory words	Few vivid words that describe subject	Too many dull words that do not appeal to senses	No attempt to use vivid sensory words
Sentences	Clear sentences; variety of sentence kinds	Mostly clear sentences; different kinds	Generally clear sentences; some variety	Some unclear sentences; little variety	Many unclear sentences; no variety	Incoherent sentences or short, choppy sentences
Conventions	Few or no errors	Several minor errors	Few serious errors	Some confusing errors	Many errors	Numerous errors

Rubric	5	4	3	2	1
Focus/Ideas	Personal narrative clearly focused; strong elaboration	Personal narrative well focused; good elaboration	Personal narrative mostly focused; some elaboration	Personal narrative often off topic; needs more elaboration	Personal narrative with no focus or elaboration
Organization/ Paragraphs	Clear sequence of events; excellent beginning, middle, end	Mostly clear sequence; good beginning, middle, end	Generally clear sequence; beginning, middle, end	Confused sequence of events; lacks beginning or ending	No attempt to put events into sequence
Voice	Sincere, engaging, unique voice	Clear, engaging voice	Sincere, pleasant voice	No clear, original voice	Uninvolved or indifferent
Word Choice	Vivid descriptive words that invoke sensory response	Vivid words that describe subject; some appeal to senses	Some vivid sensory words	Few vivid words that describe subject	No attempt to use vivid sensory words
Sentences	Clear sentences; variety of sentence kinds	Mostly clear sentences; different kinds	Generally clear sentences; some variety	Some sentences unclear; little or no variety	Incoherent sentences or short, choppy sentences
Conventions	Few or no errors	Several minor errors	Few serious errors	Many errors	Numerous errors

Rubric	4	3	2	1
Focus/Ideas	Personal narrative clearly focused; strong elaboration	Personal narrative well focused; good elaboration	Personal narrative often off topic; needs more elaboration	Personal narrative with no focus or elaboration
Organization/ Paragraphs	Clear sequence of events; good beginning, middle, end	Reasonably clear sequence; beginning, middle, end	Confused sequence of events; lacks beginning or ending	No attempt to put events into sequence
Voice	Sincere, engaging, unique voice	Pleasant voice but not compelling or unique	No clear, original voice	Uninvolved or indifferent
Word Choice	Vivid descriptive words that invoke sensory response	Some vivid words that describe subject	Few vivid words that describe subject	No attempt to use vivid sensory words
Sentences	Clear sentences; variety of sentence kinds	Mostly clear sentences with some variety	Some sentences unclear; little or no variety	Incoherent sentences or short, choppy sentences
Conventions	Few or no errors	Several minor errors	Many errors	Numerous errors

2 Rubrics

Rubric	6	5	4	3	2	1
Focus/Ideas	How-to report with strong focus; clear, complete details	How-to report well focused; clear details	How-to report with generally clear focus and details	How-to report with weak focus; few clear details	How-to report often off topic; lacks clear details	How-to report with no focus or details
Organization/ Paragraphs	Strong introduction, conclusion; steps in clear, logical order	Good introduction, conclusion; steps in logical order	Introduction, conclusion; most steps in logical order	Weak introduction and/or conclusion; some steps out of order	Missing introduction or conclusion steps in confused order	No introduction or conclusion; no attempt to order steps
Voice	Solid knowledge of topic; connects with audience	Engaging, mostly well-informed	Pleasant voice; somewhat knowledgeable	Sincere but not very knowledgeable about topic	Uncertain voice	No clear voice
Word Choice	Uses time-order words effectively	Uses time-order words well	Uses some time-order words	Uses one or two time-order words; needs more	Uses few or no time-order words	No attempt to use time-order words
Sentences	Clear, varied sentences; appropriate to form	Mostly clear, appropriate sentences; some variety	Sentences generally clear; some variety	Some sentences not appropriate; little variety	Some sentences unclear; no variety	Incoherent sentences
Conventions	Few or no errors	Several minor errors	Few serious errors	Some confusing errors	Many errors	Numerous errors

Rubric	5	4	3	2	1
Focus/Ideas	How-to report with strong focus; clear, complete details	How-to report well focused; clear details	How-to report with generally clear focus and details	How-to report often off topic; lacks clear details	How-to report with no focus or details
Organization/ Paragraphs	Strong introduction, conclusion; steps in clear, logical order	Good introduction, conclusion; steps in logical order	Introduction, conclusion; most steps in logical order	Missing introduction or conclusion; steps in confused order	No introduction or conclusion; no attempt to order steps
Voice	Solid knowledge of topic; connects with audience	Engaging, mostly well-informed	Pleasant voice; somewhat knowledgeable	Uncertain voice	No clear voice
Word Choice	Uses time-order words effectively	Uses time-order words well	Uses some time-order words	Uses few time-order words	No attempt to use time-order words
Sentences	Clear, varied sentences; appropriate to form	Mostly clear, appropriate sentences; some variety	Sentences generally clear; some variety	Some sentences unclear	Incoherent sentences
Conventions	Few or no errors	Several minor errors	Few serious errors	Many errors	Numerous errors

Rubric	4	3	2	1
Focus/Ideas	How-to report well focused; clear details	How-to report generally focused; good details	How-to report often off topic; lacks clear details	How-to report with no focus or details
Organization/ Paragraphs	Good introduction and conclusion; steps in clear, logical order	Introduction and conclusion; steps in logical order	Missing introduction or conclusion; steps in confused order	No introduction or conclusion; no attempt to order steps
Voice	Solid knowledge of topic; connects with audience	Pleasant voice but lacks some knowledge	Uncertain voice	No clear voice
Word Choice	Uses time-order words to show sequence	Uses some time-order words	Uses few time-order words	No attempt to use time-order words
Sentences	Clear, varied sentences	Mostly clear sentences	Some sentences unclear	Incoherent sentences
Conventions	Few or no errors	Several minor errors	Many errors	Numerous errors

Rubric	6	5	4	3	2	1
Focus/Ideas	Excellent, focused essay; quality details	Good, focused essay; good details	Focused essay with adequate details	Somewhat unfocused essay; needs more details	Few details and/or lack of focus in essay	Essay lacking clarity or development
Organization/ Paragraphs	Clear compare/contrast structure; easy to follow	Logical structure to compare and contrast	Mostly logical compare/contrast structure	Gaps in compare/contrast structure; hard to follow	Structure not clear	Lacks organization
Voice	Engaging, lively; shows authority	Writer engaged with subject; some authority	Writer mostly engaged and informed	Sincere but not fully engaged	Weak voice; little involvement with subject	Not engaged with subject
Word Choice	Strong verbs, clear transitions to highlight qualities	Some strong verbs; some clear transitions	Some clear verbs and transitions	One or two good verbs, transitions; needs more	Vague, repetitive verbs; few transitions	Incorrect or limited word choice
Sentences	Sentence structures varied, interesting; natural flow	Correct, interesting sentences	Correct, sometimes varied sentences	Simple sentences; lacking variety	Choppy sentences; no variety	Fragments or run-on sentences
Conventions	Few or no errors	Several minor errors	Few serious errors	Some confusing errors	Many errors	Numerous errors

Rubric	5	4	3	2	1
Focus/Ideas	Excellent, focused essay; quality details	Good, focused essay; good details	Focused essay with adequate details	Few details and/or lack of focus in essay	Essay lacking clarity or development
Organization/ Paragraphs	Clear compare/contrast structure; easy to follow	Logical structure to compare and contrast	Mostly logical compare/contrast structure	Structure not clear	Lacks organization
Voice	Engaging, lively; shows authority	Writer engaged with subject; some authority	Writer mostly engaged and informed	Weak voice; little involvement with subject	Not engaged with subject
Word Choice	Strong verbs, clear transitions to highlight qualities	Some strong verbs; some good transitions	Some clear verbs and transitions	Vague, repetitive verbs; few transitions	Incorrect or limited word choice
Sentences	Sentence structures varied, interesting; natural flow	Correct, interesting sentences	Correct, sometimes varied sentences	Choppy sentences; no variety	Fragments or run-on sentences
Conventions	Few or no errors	Several minor errors	Few serious errors	Many errors	Numerous errors

Rubric	4	3	2	1
Focus/Ideas	Excellent, focused essay; quality details	Good, focused essay; good details	Few details and/or lack of focus in essay	Essay lacking clarity or development
Organization/ Paragraphs	Clear compare/contrast structure; easy to follow	Logical structure to compare and contrast	Structure not clear	Lacks organization
Voice	Engaging, lively; shows authority	Writer engaged with subject	Weak voice	Not engaged with subject
Word Choice	Strong verbs, clear transitions to highlight qualities	Some strong verbs; some good transitions	Vague, repetitive verbs; few transitions	Incorrect or limited word choice
Sentences	Sentence structures varied, interesting; natural flow	Correct, interesting sentences	Choppy sentences; no variety	Fragments or run-on sentences
Conventions	Few or no errors	Several minor errors	Many errors	Numerous errors

Rubric	6	5	4	3	2	1
Focus/Ideas	Story focused on characters, plot, problem, solution; excellent elaboration	Story generally focused; good elaboration	Story with adequate focus and elaboration	Story sometimes unfocused; needs more good elaboration	Story often off topic; lacks elaboration	Story with no focus or elaboration
Organization/ Paragraphs	Strong beginning, middle, and end	Clear beginning, middle, and end	Reasonably clear beginning, middle, and end	Unclear beginning, middle, and end	Missing beginning, middle, and/or end	No attempt at beginning, middle, or end
Voice	Engaging, unique voice	Pleasing, generally engaging voice	Pleasant voice but not compelling or unique	Bland voice; not very engaging	No clear, original voice	Uninvolved or indifferent
Word Choice	Vivid; creates humor or tension; natural dialogue	Some vivid words that convey a mood; dialogue	Some vivid words used to create mood; some dialogue	Generally adequate but not vivid words; flat dialogue	Few vivid words; little emotion or dialogue	Vague, incorrect, dull words; no dialogue
Sentences	Clear sentences; variety of sentence kinds	Mostly clear sentences; some variety	Generally clear, varied sentences	Too many simple sentences; little variety	Some sentences unclear; no variety	Incoherent sentences or short, choppy sentences
Conventions	Few or no errors	Several minor errors	Few serious errors	Some confusing errors	Many errors	Numerous errors

Rubric	5	4	3	2	1
Focus/Ideas	Story focused on characters, plot, problem, solution; excellent elaboration	Story generally focused; good elaboration	Story with adequate focus and elaboration	Story often off topic; lacks good elaboration	Story with no focus or elaboration
Organization/ Paragraphs	Engaging beginning, middle, and end	Clear beginning, middle, and end	Reasonably clear beginning, middle, and end	Unclear beginning, middle, and end	No attempt at beginning, middle, or end
Voice	Engaging, unique voice	Pleasing, generally engaging voice	Pleasant voice but not compelling or unique	No clear, original voice	Uninvolved or indifferent
Word Choice	Vivid; creates humor or tension; natural dialogue	Some vivid words that convey a mood; dialogue	Some vivid words used to create mood; some dialogue	Few vivid words; little emotion or dialogue	Vague, incorrect, dull words; no dialogue
Sentences	Clear sentences; variety of sentence kinds	Mostly clear sentences; some variety	Generally clear, varied sentences	Some sentences unclear; little or no variety	Incoherent sentences or short, choppy sentences
Conventions	Few or no errors	Several minor errors	Few serious errors	Many errors	Numerous errors

Rubric	4	3	2	1
Focus/Ideas	Story focused on characters, plot, problem, solution; excellent elaboration	Story generally focused; good elaboration	Story often off topic; lacks good elaboration	Story with no focus or elaboration
Organization/ Paragraphs	Clear beginning, middle, and end	Reasonably clear beginning, middle, and end	Unclear beginning, middle, and end	No attempt at beginning, middle, or end
Voice	Engaging, unique voice	Pleasant voice but not compelling or unique	No clear, original voice	Uninvolved or indifferent
Word Choice	Vivid; creates humor or tension; natural dialogue	Some vivid words that convey a mood; dialogue	Few vivid words; little emotion or dialogue	Vague, incorrect, dull words; no dialogue
Sentences	Clear sentences; variety of sentence kinds	Mostly clear sentences; some variety	Some sentences unclear; little or no variety	Incoherent sentences or short, choppy sentences
Conventions	Few or no errors	Several minor errors	Many errors	Numerous errors

Rubric	6	5	4	3	2	1
Focus/Ideas	Essay with clearly stated opinion and strong reasons	Essay with stated opinion and good reasons	Essay with generally clear opinion and some good reasons	Essay with vague opinion and weak reasons	Essay lacking either opinion or sufficient reasons	Essay with no opinion or reasons
Organization/ Paragraphs	Reasons in clear, logical order, strongest one last	Reasons in logical order, strongest one last	Reasons in mostly logical order	Reasons not in logical order	Reasons in no discernible order	Lacks reasons or order
Voice	Serious, persuasive	Mostly serious, persuasive	Reasonably serious, persuasive	Somewhat serious but not very persuasive	Not involved enough with topic	Not involved at all with topic
Word Choice	Uses persuasive words and vivid adjectives expertly	Uses persuasive words and vivid adjectives well	Uses some persuasive words, vivid adjectives	Too many words that lack persuasive power or vividness	Uses few persuasive words or vivid adjectives	Incorrect or limited choice of words; lacks persuasive words
Sentences	Well-constructed, varied sentences	Good, varied sentences	Correct sentences; some variety	Mostly simple sentences; little variety	Too many short, choppy sentences; no variety	Mostly fragments, run-on sentences
Conventions	Few or no errors	Several minor errors	Few serious errors	Some confusing errors	Many errors	Numerous errors

Rubric	5	4	3	2	1
Focus/Ideas	Essay with clearly stated opinion and strong reasons	Essay with stated opinion and good reasons	Essay with generally clear opinion and some good reasons	Essay with vague opinion and few reasons	Essay with no opinion or reasons
Organization/ Paragraphs	Reasons in clear, logical order, strongest one last	Reasons in logical order, strongest one last	Reasons in mostly logical order	Reasons in no discernible order	Lacks reasons or order
Voice	Serious, persuasive	Mostly serious, persuasive	Reasonably serious, persuasive	Not involved enough with topic	Not involved at all with topic
Word Choice	Uses persuasive words and vivid adjectives expertly	Uses many persuasive words; some vivid adjectives	Uses some persuasive words, vivid adjectives	Uses few persuasive words or vivid adjectives	Incorrect or limited choice of words; lacks persuasive words
Sentences	Well-constructed, varied sentences	Good, varied sentences	Correct sentences; some variety	Too many short, choppy sentences; little variety	Mostly fragments, run-on sentences
Conventions	Few or no errors	Several minor errors	Few serious errors	Many errors	Numerous errors

Rubric	4	3	2	1
Focus/Ideas	Essay with clear opinion and strong reasons	Essay with stated opinion and good reasons	Essay with vague opinion and few reasons	Essay with no opinion or reasons
Organization/ Paragraphs	Reasons in logical order, strongest one last	Reasons in order, strongest one last	Reasons in no discernible order	Lacks reasons or order
Voice	Serious, persuasive	Mostly serious, persuasive	Not involved enough with topic	Not involved at all with topic
Word Choice	Uses persuasive words and vivid adjectives expertly	Uses some persuasive words and vivid adjectives	Uses few persuasive words or vivid adjectives	Incorrect or limited choice of words; lacks persuasive words
Sentences	Well-constructed, varied sentences	Good sentences; some variety	Too many short, choppy sentences; little variety	Mostly fragments, run-on sentences
Conventions	Few or no errors	Several minor errors	Many errors	Numerous errors

Rubric	6	5	4	3	2	1
Focus/Ideas	Well-focused report with strong thesis and support	Focused report with good thesis and support	Generally focused report; adequate support	Report with unclear focus; some details	Report sometimes off topic; needs more support	Report lacking focus or thesis statement
Organization/ Paragraphs	Logical order; no gaps	Order mostly logical; one or two minor gaps	Order generally logical; few gaps	Order not always logical; some gaps	Confused order; some major gaps	Lacks organization
Voice	Engaging, interested, well-informed	Involved with subject, informative	Generally informed and engaging	Somewhat interested, informed; not involved enough	Involved with subject at times; not informative	Not involved with subject; no distinct voice
Word Choice	Vivid, precise word choice	Words mostly precise, often vivid	Accurate words; some vivid words	Some accurate words; few vivid words	Some vague, repetitive, or incorrect words	Incorrect or limited word choice
Sentences	Structures clear, varied, smooth	Controlled, correct structures; good variety	Mostly correct sentences; some variety	Too many simple structures; little variety	Choppy sentences; lacks variety	Fragments, run-on sentences
Conventions	Few or no errors	Several minor errors	Few serious errors	Some confusing errors	Many errors	Numerous errors

Rubric	5	4	3	2	1
Focus/Ideas	Well-focused report with strong thesis and support	Focused report with good thesis and support	Generally focused report; adequate support	Report sometimes off topic; needs more support	Report lacking focus or thesis statement
Organization/ Paragraphs	Logical order; no gaps	Order mostly logical; one or two minor gaps	Order generally logical; few gaps	Confused order; some gaps	Lacks organization
Voice	Engaging, interested, well-informed	Involved with subject, informative	Generally informed and engaging	Involved with subject at times; not informative	Not involved with subject; no distinct voice
Word Choice	Vivid, precise word choice	Words mostly precise, often vivid	Accurate words; some vivid words	Some vague, repetitive, or incorrect words	Incorrect or limited word choice
Sentences	Structures clear, varied, smooth	Controlled, correct structures; good variety	Mostly correct sentences; some variety	Choppy sentences; lacks variety	Fragments, run-on sentences
Conventions	Few or no errors	Several minor errors	Few serious errors	Many errors	Numerous errors

Rubric	4	3	2	1
Focus/Ideas	Well-focused report with strong thesis and support	Focused report with good thesis and support	Report sometimes off topic; needs more support	Report lacking focus or thesis statement
Organization/ Paragraphs	Logical order; no gaps	Order mostly logical; few gaps	Order with some gaps	Lacks organization
Voice	Engaging, interested, well-informed	Involved with subject; informative	Involved with subject at times; not informative	Not involved with subject; no distinct voice
Word Choice	Vivid, precise word choice	Accurate word choice	Some vague, repetitive, or incorrect words	Incorrect or limited word choice
Sentences	Structures clear, varied, smooth	Controlled, correct structures; some variety	Choppy sentences; lacks variety	Fragments, run-on sentences
Conventions	Few or no errors	Several minor errors	Many errors	Numerous errors

Weekly Rubrics

Rubric	6	5	4	3	2	1
Focus/Ideas	Vivid description of experience; strong supporting details	Good description of experience; good details	Adequate description of experience; some details	Sketchy description of experience; few details	Description that strays off topic; few details	No description; lacks clarity and development
Organization/ Paragraphs	Events in clear, logical order; uses sequence words well	Events in logical order; uses sequence words	Events in mostly logical order; some sequence words	Events out of order at times; few sequence words	Events not arranged logically; no sequence words	Lacks organization
Voice	Written in first person; writer enthusiastic about memory	Mostly in first person; writer involved with topic	Generally in first person; writer interested in topic	Lapses in use of first person; writer somewhat involved	Writer not very involved	Writer not involved at all
Word Choice	Strong verbs and adjectives that show, not tell	Mostly strong verbs and adjectives that show, not tell	Some strong verbs and adjectives	Few strong verbs or adjectives; needs more	Vague, repetitive, or incorrect word choice	Incorrect or limited word choice
Sentences	Uses variety of sentences correctly, effectively	Correct sentences; good variety	Mostly correct sentences; some variety	Many simple sentences; little variety	Only simple sentences; no variety	Fragments or run-on sentences
Conventions	Excellent control	Good control with few errors	Some errors	Some confusing errors	Many errors, some serious	Numerous serious errors

Rubric	5	4	3	2	1
Focus/Ideas	Vivid description of experience; strong supporting details	Good description of experience; good details	Adequate description of experience; some details	Poor description of experience; few details	No description; lacks clarity and development
Organization/ Paragraphs	Events in clear, logical order; uses sequence words well	Events in logical order; uses sequence words	Events in mostly logical order; some sequence words	Events not arranged logically; no sequence words	Lacks organization
Voice	Written in first person; writer enthusiastic about memory	Mostly in first person; writer involved with topic	Generally in first person; writer interested in topic	Writer not very involved	Writer not involved at all
Word Choice	Strong verbs and adjectives that show, not tell	Mostly strong verbs and adjectives that show, not tell	Some strong verbs and adjectives	Vague, repetitive, or incorrect word choice	Incorrect or limited word choice
Sentences	Uses variety of sentences correctly, effectively	Correct sentences; good variety	Mostly correct sentences; some variety	Only simple sentences; no variety	Fragments or run-on sentences
Conventions	Excellent control	Good control with few errors	Some errors	Many errors, some serious	Numerous serious errors

Rubric	4	3	2	1
Focus/Ideas	Vivid description of experience; many supporting details	Good description of experience; some details	Poor description of experience; few details	No description; lacks clarity and development
Organization/ Paragraphs	Logical sequence of events; uses sequence words	Events mostly in logical order; some sequence words	Events not arranged logically; no sequence words	Lacks organization
Voice	Written in first person; writer enthusiastic about memory	Mostly in first person; writer somewhat involved	Writer not very involved	Writer not involved at all
Word Choice	Strong verbs and adjectives that show, not tell	Some strong verbs and adjectives	Vague, repetitive, or incorrect word choice	Incorrect or limited word choice
Sentences	Uses variety of sentences correctly	Some sentence variety	Only simple sentences; no variety	Fragments or run-on sentences
Conventions	Excellent control	Reasonable control with few errors	Many errors	Numerous serious errors

Rubric	6	5	4	3	2	1
Focus/Ideas	Vivid character sketch; many actions and traits described	Good character sketch; good descriptive details	Character sketch with adequate details	Character sketch sometimes off topic; some details	Few revealing details about person in character sketch	No focus on character; no descriptive details
Organization/ Paragraphs	Key traits fully developed with details/ examples	Development of key traits orderly and logical	Key traits developed in mostly logical order	Some key traits developed; order not always logical	Few traits; details not arranged logically	Lacks organization; only one trait
Voice	Sincere, engaging; writer cares about subject	Sincere; writer involved with subject	Generally sincere and interested in subject	Somewhat interested in subject	Tries to deal with subject but not very involved	Writer not involved with subject
Word Choice	Character traits conveyed through specific words	Character traits portrayed through clear language	Character traits conveyed using mostly clear language	Language too general to portray character traits well	Some vague, repetitive, or incorrect words	Incorrect or limited word choice
Sentences	Well constructed; varied to add interest	Mostly well constructed and varied	Correct sentences; some variety	Control over simple sentences; little variety	Choppy sentences; lacks variation	Fragments or run-on sentences
Conventions	Excellent control	Good control with few errors	Some errors	Some confusing errors	Many errors, some serious	Numerous serious errors

Rubric	5	4	3	2	1
Focus/Ideas	Vivid character sketch; many actions and traits described	Good character sketch; good descriptive details	Character sketch with adequate details	Few revealing details about person in character sketch	No focus on character; no descriptive details
Organization/ Paragraphs	Key traits fully developed with details/examples	Development of key traits orderly and logical	Key traits developed in mostly logical order	Few traits; details not arranged logically	Lacks organization; only one trait
Voice	Sincere, engaging; writer cares about subject	Sincere; writer involved with subject	Generally sincere and interested in subject	Tries to deal with subject but not very involved	Writer not involved with subject
Word Choice	Character traits conveyed through specific words	Character traits portrayed through clear language	Character traits conveyed using mostly clear language	Some vague, repetitive, or incorrect words	Incorrect or limited word choice
Sentences	Well constructed; varied to add interest	Mostly well constructed and varied	Correct sentences; some variety	Choppy sentences; lacks variation	Fragments or run-on sentences
Conventions	Excellent control	Good control with few errors	Some errors	Many errors, some serious	Numerous serious errors

Rubric	4	3	2	1
Focus/Ideas	Vivid character sketch; many actions and traits described	Good character sketch; good descriptive details	Few revealing details about person in character sketch	No focus on character; no descriptive details
Organization/ Paragraphs	Key traits fully developed with details/examples	Development of key traits orderly and logical	Few traits; details not arranged logically	Lacks organization; only one trait
Voice	Sincere, engaging; writer cares about subject	Writer involved with subject	Tries to deal with subject but not very involved	Writer not involved with subject
Word Choice	Character traits conveyed through specific words	Character traits portrayed through clear language	Some vague, repetitive, or incorrect words	Incorrect or limited word choice
Sentences	Well constructed; varied to add interest	Generally well constructed and varied	Choppy sentences; lacks variation	Fragments or run-on sentences
Conventions	Excellent control	Reasonable control with few errors	Many errors	Numerous serious errors

Rubric

Rubric	6	5	4	3	2	1
Focus/Ideas	Vivid journal entry; many events and details included	Fairly vivid journal entry; good supporting details	Mostly clear journal entry; some supporting details	Journal entry somewhat unfocused; needs more details	Journal entry with few details about events	Journal entry lacking clarity and development
Organization/ Paragraphs	Events laid out clearly and logically	Events arranged logically	Order of events generally clear	Order of events unclear at times	Events and details not arranged logically	Lacks organization
Voice	Original and interesting; stands out from others	Writer involved with subject; engages reader	Shows some interest in subject and some originality	Writer involved at times	Tries to deal with subject but does not get very involved	Writer not involved with subject
Word Choice	Events and details conveyed through specific words	Events and details portrayed through clear language	Events and details conveyed using mostly clear language	Language too general to portray events and details well	Some vague, repetitive, or incorrect words	Incorrect, dull, limited word choice
Sentences	Sentences of different lengths and structures	Some different lengths and structures	Control over simple sentence structure	Too many simple sentences; little variety	Choppy sentences; lacks variation	Fragments or run-on sentences
Conventions	Excellent control	Good control with few errors	Some errors	Some confusing errors	Many errors, some serious	Numerous serious errors

Rubric

Rubric	5	4	3	2	1
Focus/Ideas	Vivid journal entry; many events and details included	Fairly vivid journal entry; adequate supporting details	Mostly clear journal entry; some supporting details	Journal entry with few details about events	Journal entry lacking clarity and development
Organization/ Paragraphs	Events laid out clearly and logically	Events arranged logically	Order of events generally clear	Events and details not arranged logically	Lacks organization
Voice	Original and interesting; stands out from others	Writer involved with subject; engages reader	Shows interest in subject and originality	Tries to deal with subject but does not get very involved	Writer not involved with subject
Word Choice	Events and details conveyed through specific words	Events and details portrayed through clear language	Mostly adequate language to portray events, details	Some vague, repetitive, or incorrect words	Incorrect or limited word choice
Sentences	Sentences of different lengths and structures	Some different lengths and structures	Control over simple sentence structure	Choppy sentences; lacks variation	Fragments or run-on sentences
Conventions	Excellent control	Good control with few errors	Some errors	Many errors, some serious	Numerous serious errors

Rubric

Rubric	4	3	2	1
Focus/Ideas	Vivid journal entry; many events and details included	Fairly vivid journal entry; some supporting details	Journal entry with few details about events	Journal entry lacking clarity and development
Organization/ Paragraphs	Events laid out clearly and logically	Order of events generally clear and logical	Events and details not arranged logically	Lacks organization
Voice	Original and interesting; stands out from others	Writer involved with subject; engages reader	Tries to deal with subject but does not get very involved	Writer not involved with subject
Word Choice	Events and details conveyed through specific words	Events and details portrayed through clear language	Some vague, repetitive, or incorrect words	Incorrect or limited word choice
Sentences	Sentences of different lengths and structures	Control over simple sentence structure	Choppy sentences; lacks variation	Fragments or run-on sentences
Conventions	Excellent control	Reasonable control with few errors	Many errors	Numerous serious errors

Rubric	6	5	4	3	2	1
Focus/Ideas	Clear problem/solution; strong development	Mostly clear problem/solution; good development	Fairly clear problem/solution; adequate development	Problem/solution; some development	No clear problem/solution; little development	No problem or solution; lacks development
Organization/ Paragraphs	Clear, logical order; three strong supporting details	Logical order; three good supporting details	Order generally clear; only two supporting details	Order somewhat confused; one or two supporting details	Only one supporting detail; no order	Lacks organization and support
Voice	Sincere, individual; writer deeply involved with subject	Sincere; writer involved with subject	Sincere; shows some involvement and individuality	Confident at times; somewhat involved	Tries to deal with subject but does not get very involved	Writer not involved with subject
Word Choice	Argument convincing; uses specific words	Argument mostly persuasive; clear language	Argument fairly persuasive; some specific words	Lacks specific words needed to persuade	Some vague, repetitive, or incorrect words	Incorrect or limited word choice
Sentences	Well constructed; varied to add interest	Mostly well constructed and varied	Correct sentences; some variety	Control over simple sentences; little variety	Choppy sentences; lacks variation	Fragments or run-on sentences
Conventions	Excellent control	Good control with few errors	Some errors	Some confusing errors	Many errors, some serious	Numerous serious errors

Rubric	5	4	3	2	1
Focus/Ideas	Clear problem/solution; strong development	Mostly clear problem/solution; good development	Fairly clear problem/solution; adequate development	No clear problem/solution; little development	No problem or solution; lacks development
Organization/ Paragraphs	Clear order; three good supporting details	Logical order; three supporting details	Order generally clear; only two supporting details	Only one supporting detail; no order	Lacks organization and support
Voice	Sincere, individual; writer deeply involved with subject	Sincere; writer involved with subject	Sincere; shows some involvement and individuality	Tries to deal with subject but does not get very involved	Writer not involved with subject
Word Choice	Argument convincing; uses specific words	Argument mostly persuasive; clear language	Argument fairly persuasive; some specific words	Some vague, repetitive, or incorrect words	Incorrect or limited word choice
Sentences	Well constructed; varied to add interest	Mostly well constructed and varied	Correct sentences; some variety	Choppy sentences; lacks variation	Fragments or run-on sentences
Conventions	Excellent control	Good control with few errors	Some errors	Many errors, some serious	Numerous serious errors

Rubric	4	3	2	1
Focus/Ideas	Clear problem/solution; strong development	Fairly clear problem/solution; good development	No clear problem/solution; little development	No problem or solution; lacks development
Organization/ Paragraphs	Clear order; three supporting details	Order generally clear; only two supporting details	Only one or two supporting details	Lacks organization and support
Voice	Sincere, individual; writer deeply involved with subject	Sincere; writer involved with subject	Tries to deal with subject but does not get very involved	Writer not involved with subject
Word Choice	Argument convincing; uses specific words	Argument fairly persuasive; clear language	Some vague, repetitive, or incorrect words	Incorrect or limited word choice
Sentences	Varied structures; adds interest	Control over simple sentence structure	Choppy sentences; lacks variation	Fragments or run-on sentences
Conventions	Excellent control	Reasonable control with few errors	Many errors	Numerous serious errors

Rubric	6	5	4	3	2	1
Focus/Ideas	Vivid narrative with excellent elaboration	Mostly vivid narrative; good elaboration	Fairly vivid narrative; adequate elaboration	Narrative at times unfocused, with little elaboration	Weak elaboration and/or lack of focus in narrative	Narrative lacking elaboration and development
Organization/ Paragraphs	Strong beginning; clear sequence of events	Good beginning; sequence logical	Adequate beginning; sequence mostly logical	Weak beginning; some events out of sequence	Beginning missing or distracting; sequence not clear	No clear beginning or sequence of events
Voice	Sense of writer's personality clearly conveyed	Writer engaged with subject; shows personality	Generally engaged; shows some personality	Writer somewhat involved; hint of personality	Writer not very engaged with subject	Writer not engaged with subject at all
Word Choice	Many vivid verbs and sharp descriptions	Mostly vivid verbs; clear descriptions	Some vivid verbs; some good descriptions	Adequate language with little life or color	Vague, repetitive, or incorrect words	Incorrect or limited word choice
Sentences	Varied, well-crafted sentences	Generally well-crafted, varied structures	Correct sentences; some variety	Simple sentences; little variety	Choppy sentences; lacks variation	Fragments or run-on sentences
Conventions	Excellent control	Good control with few errors	Some errors	Some confusing errors	Many errors, some serious	Numerous serious errors

Rubric	5	4	3	2	1
Focus/Ideas	Vivid narrative with excellent elaboration	Mostly vivid narrative; good elaboration	Fairly vivid narrative; adequate elaboration	Narrative with little elaboration and/or lack of focus	Narrative lacking elaboration and development
Organization/ Paragraphs	Strong beginning; clear sequence of events	Good beginning; sequence logical	Adequate beginning; sequence mostly logical	Beginning not engaging; sequence not clear	No clear beginning or sequence of events
Voice	Sense of writer's personality clearly conveyed	Writer engaged with subject; shows personality	Generally engaged; shows some personality	Writer not very engaged with subject	Writer not engaged with subject at all
Word Choice	Many vivid verbs and sharp descriptions	Mostly vivid verbs; clear descriptions	Some vivid verbs; some good descriptions	Vague, repetitive, or incorrect words	Incorrect or limited word choice
Sentences	Varied, well-crafted sentences	Generally well-crafted, varied structures	Correct sentences; some variety	Choppy sentences; lacks variation	Fragments or run-on sentences
Conventions	Excellent control	Good control with few errors	Some errors	Many errors, some serious	Numerous serious errors

Rubric	4	3	2	1
Focus/Ideas	Vivid narrative with excellent elaboration	Fairly vivid narrative; adequate elaboration	Narrative with little elaboration and/or lack of focus	Narrative lacking elaboration and development
Organization/ Paragraphs	Strong beginning; clear sequence of events	Good beginning; sequence logical	Beginning not engaging; sequence not clear	No clear beginning or sequence of events
Voice	Sense of writer's personality clearly conveyed	Writer engaged with subject; shows personality	Writer not very engaged with subject	Writer not engaged with subject at all
Word Choice	Many vivid verbs and sharp descriptions	Some vivid verbs and sharp descriptions	Vague, repetitive, or incorrect words	Incorrect or limited word choice
Sentences	Varied, well-crafted sentences	Control over simple sentence structure	Choppy sentences; lacks variation	Fragments or run-on sentences
Conventions	Excellent control	Reasonable control with few errors	Many errors	Numerous serious errors

Rubric	6	5	4	3	2	1
Focus/Ideas	Clear, brief directions; all crucial information	Clear directions; no extra information	Fairly clear directions; little extra information	Directions sometimes unclear; some extra information	Directions that stray; some misleading information	No directions; lacks clarity and development
Organization/ Paragraphs	Steps in logical order and easy to follow	Steps in mostly logical order; no missteps	Steps in reasonably logical order; few missteps	Some steps out of order; somewhat hard to follow	Steps not arranged logically; some missteps	Lacks organization; many errors
Voice	Engaging, lively, and knowledgeable	Mostly knowledgeable; engages reader	Generally informed and involved with subject	Lacks knowledge; little involvement	Tries to deal with subject but does not get very involved	Writer not involved with subject
Word Choice	Clear, specific words; uses time-order words well	Uses clear language and good time-order words	Generally clear language; some time-order words	Language often too general; few time-order words	Some vague, repetitive, or incorrect words	Incorrect or limited word choice
Sentences	Structures appropriate; aids clarity	Structures generally appropriate, clear	Fairly clear, appropriate structures	Structures not always clear or appropriate	Choppy sentences; some incorrect structures	Fragments or run-on sentences
Conventions	Excellent control	Good control with few errors	Reasonable control; some errors	Some confusing errors	Many errors	Numerous errors

Rubric	5	4	3	2	1
Focus/Ideas	Clear, brief directions; all crucial information	Clear directions; no extra information	Fairly clear directions; little extra information	Directions that stray; some misleading information	No directions; lacks clarity and development
Organization/ Paragraphs	Steps in logical order and easy to follow	Steps in mostly logical order; no missteps	Steps in fairly logical order; few missteps	Steps not arranged logically; some missteps	Lacks organization; many errors
Voice	Engaging, lively, and knowledgeable	Mostly knowledgeable; engages reader	Generally informed and involved with subject	Tries to deal with subject but does not get very involved	Writer not involved with subject
Word Choice	Clear, specific words; uses time-order words well	Uses clear language and good time-order words	Generally clear language; some time-order words	Some vague, repetitive, or incorrect words	Incorrect or limited word choice
Sentences	Structures appropriate; aids clarity	Structures generally appropriate, clear	Fairly clear, appropriate structures	Choppy sentences; some incorrect structures	Fragments or run-on sentences
Conventions	Excellent control	Good control with few errors	Reasonable control; some errors	Many errors	Numerous errors

Rubric	4	3	2	1
Focus/Ideas	Clear, brief directions; all crucial information	Fairly clear directions; no extra information	Directions that stray; some misleading information	No directions; lacks clarity and development
Organization/ Paragraphs	Steps in order and easy to follow	Steps reasonably logical; few missteps	Steps not arranged logically; some missteps	Lacks organization; many errors
Voice	Engaging, lively, and knowledgeable	Mostly knowledgeable; engages reader	Tries to deal with subject but does not get very involved	Writer not involved with subject
Word Choice	Clear, specific words; uses time-order words well	Uses clear language and time-order words	Some vague, repetitive, or incorrect words	Incorrect or limited word choice
Sentences	Structures appropriate; aids clarity	Structures generally appropriate, clear	Choppy sentences; some incorrect structures	Fragments or run-on sentences
Conventions	Excellent control	Reasonable control with few errors	Many errors	Numerous errors

Rubric	6	5	4	3	2	1
Focus/Ideas	Convincing; clear hypothesis; strong supporting details	Mostly clear hypothesis; good supporting details	Adequate hypothesis; some good supporting details	Hypothesis somewhat unclear; some supporting details	Vague hypothesis; few supporting details	Lacks clarity and development
Organization/Paragraphs	Logical, orderly argument; uses transitions effectively	Logical argument; some transitions	Generally logical argument; some transitions	Argument with lapses in logic; few transitions	Poor or limited organization; no transitions	Lacks organization and support
Voice	Authoritative, individual; stands out from others	Engaging and usually convincing	Generally engaging and persuasive	Not very engaging; does not stand out	Not authoritative or individual	Writer not involved; no distinct voice
Word Choice	Uses specific words to make convincing argument	Uses clear language to make persuasive argument	Adequate language; makes fairly persuasive argument	Too many general words; little persuasive power	Some vague, repetitive, or incorrect words	Incorrect or limited word choice
Sentences	Structures varied to add interest; smooth connections	Some varied structures and smooth connections	Control over simple sentence structures; some connections	Lacks varied structures; few connections	Choppy sentences; no connections	Fragments or run-on sentences
Conventions	Excellent control	Good control with few errors	Reasonable control; some errors	Some confusing errors	Many errors	Numerous errors

Rubric	5	4	3	2	1
Focus/Ideas	Convincing; clear hypothesis; strong supporting details	Mostly clear hypothesis; good supporting details	Adequate hypothesis; some good supporting details	Vague hypothesis; few supporting details	Lacks clarity and development
Organization/Paragraphs	Logical, orderly argument; uses transitions effectively	Logical argument; some transitions	Generally logical argument; some transitions	Poor or limited organization; no transitions	Lacks organization and support
Voice	Authoritative, individual; stands out from others	Engaging and usually convincing	Generally engaging and persuasive	Not authoritative or individual	Writer not involved; no distinct voice
Word Choice	Uses specific words to make convincing argument	Uses clear language to make persuasive argument	Adequate language; makes fairly persuasive argument	Some vague, repetitive, or incorrect words	Incorrect or limited word choice
Sentences	Structures varied to add interest; smooth connections	Some varied structures and smooth connections	Control over simple sentence structures; some connections	Choppy sentences; no connections	Fragments or run-on sentences
Conventions	Excellent control	Good control with few errors	Reasonable control; some errors	Many errors	Numerous errors

Rubric	4	3	2	1
Focus/Ideas	Clear hypothesis; strong supporting details	Fairly clear hypothesis; good supporting details	Vague hypothesis; few supporting details	Lacks clarity and development
Organization/Paragraphs	Logical, orderly argument	Reasonably logical argument	Poor or limited organization	Lacks organization and support
Voice	Authoritative, individual; stands out from others	Engaging and usually convincing	Not authoritative or individual	Writer not involved; no distinct voice
Word Choice	Argument made convincing through specific words	Argument made persuasive with clear language	Some vague, repetitive, or incorrect words	Incorrect or limited word choice
Sentences	Structures varied to add interest; smooth connections	Control over simple sentence structures; some connections	Choppy sentences; no connections	Fragments or run-on sentences
Conventions	Excellent control	Reasonable control with few errors	Many errors	Numerous errors

Rubric	6	5	4	3	2	1
Focus/Ideas	Clear, focused letter; appropriate, engaging content	Focused letter; appropriate content	Mostly focused letter; most content appropriate	Letter with unclear focus; some inappropriate content	Letter that strays from topic	Not a letter; lacks clarity and development
Organization/ Paragraphs	Correct letter format; ideas well organized	Correct letter format; organized ideas	Generally correct letter format; ideas mostly organized	Missing some letter elements; ideas disorganized at times	Missing many letter elements; ideas disorganized	No letter format; lacks organization
Voice	Writer friendly, engaging; involved with subject	Writer friendly, involved with subject	Writer generally friendly and involved with subject	Tries to be involved with subject; not very engaging	Writer not very involved with subject	Writer not involved with subject
Word Choice	Communicates clearly through specific, vivid words	Uses clear, specific language	Some specific language	Language adequate but lacks color	Some vague, repetitive, or incorrect words	Incorrect or limited word choice
Sentences	Good control over variety of sentence structures	Smooth sentence structures; some variety	Reasonable control over different sentence structures	Mostly simple sentences; little variety	Choppy sentences	Fragments or run-ons
Conventions	Excellent control	Good control with few errors	Reasonable control; some errors	Some confusing errors	Many errors	Numerous errors

Rubric	5	4	3	2	1
Focus/Ideas	Clear, focused letter; appropriate, engaging content	Focused letter; appropriate content	Mostly focused letter; most content appropriate	Letter that strays from topic at times	Not a letter; lacks clarity and development
Organization/ Paragraphs	Correct letter format; ideas well organized	Correct letter format; organized ideas	Generally correct letter format; ideas mostly organized	Missing letter elements; ideas disorganized	No letter format; lacks organization
Voice	Writer friendly, engaging; involved with subject	Writer friendly, involved with subject	Writer generally friendly and involved with subject	Writer not very involved with subject	Writer not involved with subject
Word Choice	Communicates clearly through specific, vivid words	Uses clear, specific language	Some specific language	Some vague, repetitive, or incorrect words	Incorrect or limited word choice
Sentences	Control over sentence structures; variety	Smooth sentence structures; some variety	Reasonable control over sentence structures	Choppy sentences	Fragments or run-ons
Conventions	Excellent control	Good control with few errors	Reasonable control; some errors	Many errors	Numerous errors

Rubric	4	3	2	1
Focus/Ideas	Clear, focused letter; appropriate, engaging content	Focused letter; most content appropriate	Letter that strays from topic at times	Not a letter; lacks clarity and development
Organization/ Paragraphs	Correct letter format; ideas well organized	Mostly correct letter format; organized ideas	Missing letter elements; disorganized ideas	No letter format; lacks organization
Voice	Writer friendly, engaging; involved with subject	Writer generally involved with subject	Writer not very involved with subject	Writer not involved with subject
Word Choice	Communicates clearly through specific words	Uses clear language	Some vague, repetitive, or incorrect words	Incorrect or limited word choice
Sentences	Control over sentence structures; variety	Control over simple sentence structures	Choppy sentences	Fragments or run-ons
Conventions	Excellent control	Reasonable control with few errors	Many errors	Numerous errors

16 Rubrics

Rubric	6	5	4	3	2	1
Focus/Ideas	Interview distinct throughout; strong support for ideas	Focus in interview maintained; good supporting details	Adequate focus in interview; some supporting details	Interview occasionally unfocused; needs more support	Some meandering in interview; ideas unsubstantiated	Interview lacking clarity and development
Organization/ Paragraphs	Correct use of Q&A format; ideas logically arranged	Clear format; ideas easy to follow	Format mostly correct; most ideas easy to follow	Some errors in Q&A format; some ideas hard to follow	Ideas not arranged logically	Lacks organization; no dialogue
Voice	Unique; distinct and engaging characters	Actively involved with characters; engages reader	Mostly involved with characters but not unique	Sincere but indistinct; uninteresting characters	Attempts dialogue but not very involved with characters	Writer not involved with characters
Word Choice	Theme and character conveyed through specific words	Character traits portrayed through clear language	Character traits conveyed through mostly clear language	Language too general to convey character traits well	Some vague, repetitive, or incorrect words	Incorrect or limited word choice
Sentences	Structures varied and natural-sounding	Good variety of structures; mostly natural	Correct sentences; some variety	Too many simple sentences; little variety	Choppy sentences; lacks variety	Fragments or run-ons
Conventions	Excellent control	Good control with few errors	Reasonable control; some errors	Some confusing errors	Many errors	Numerous errors

Rubric	5	4	3	2	1
Focus/Ideas	Interview distinct throughout; strong support for ideas	Focus in interview maintained; good supporting details	Adequate focus in interview; some supporting details	Some meandering in interview; ideas unsubstantiated	Interview lacking clarity and development
Organization/ Paragraphs	Correct use of Q&A format; ideas logically arranged	Clear format; ideas easy to follow	Q&A format mostly correct; most ideas easy to follow	Ideas not arranged logically	Lacks organization; no dialogue
Voice	Unique; distinct and engaging characters	Actively involved with characters; interesting	Mostly involved with characters but not unique	Attempts dialogue but not very involved with characters	Writer not involved with characters
Word Choice	Theme and character conveyed through specific words	Character traits portrayed through clear language	Character traits conveyed through mostly clear language	Some vague, repetitive, or incorrect words	Incorrect or limited word choice
Sentences	Structures varied and natural-sounding	Good variety of structures; mostly natural	Correct sentences; some variety	Choppy sentences; lacks variety	Fragments or run-ons
Conventions	Excellent control	Good control with few errors	Reasonable control; some errors	Many errors	Numerous errors

Rubric	4	3	2	1
Focus/Ideas	Interview distinct throughout; strong support for ideas	Focus in interview well maintained; some supporting details	Some meandering in interview; ideas unsubstantiated	Interview lacking clarity and development
Organization/ Paragraphs	Correct use of Q&A format; ideas logically arranged	Clear format; ideas easy to follow	Ideas not arranged logically	Lacks organization; no dialogue
Voice	Unique; distinct and engaging characters	Writer involved with characters	Attempts dialogue but not very involved with characters	Writer not involved with characters
Word Choice	Theme and character conveyed through specific words	Character traits portrayed through clear language	Some vague, repetitive, or incorrect words	Incorrect or limited word choice
Sentences	Structures varied and natural	Control over simple sentence structures	Choppy sentences; lacks variety	Fragments or run-ons
Conventions	Excellent control	Reasonable control with few errors	Many errors	Numerous errors

Rubric	6	5	4	3	2	1
Focus/Ideas	Clear, succinct explanation; strong supporting details	Mostly clear explanation; good supporting details	Generally clear explanation; some supporting details	Explanation unclear at times; needs more support	Explanation with few details and/or lack of focus	Explanation with lack of clarity and development
Organization/ Paragraphs	Uses paragraphs with clear structure and transitions	Paragraphs with logical structure; uses transitions	Reasonable paragraph structure; some transitions	Attempt at structure; not enough paragraphs or transitions	No paragraphs; structure not clear	No noticeable organization
Voice	Writer engaged; shows authority over subject	Writer generally engaged and authoritative	Writer involved with subject; shows some authority	Writer not fully involved; shows little authority	Weak voice; little writer involvement	Writer not engaged with subject
Word Choice	Uses specific words for clarity and interest	Uses clear words and some vivid images	Words mostly clear; some interesting images	Language adequate but little color or precision	Vague, repetitive, or incorrect words	Incorrect or limited word choice
Sentences	Sentence structures appropriate, varied, interesting	Mostly well-crafted sentences; good variety	Correct sentences; some variety	Mostly correct, simple sentences; little variety	Choppy sentences; no variety	Fragments or run-ons
Conventions	Excellent control and accuracy	Good control with few errors	Reasonable control; some errors	Some confusing errors	Many errors	Numerous errors

Rubric	5	4	3	2	1
Focus/Ideas	Clear, succinct explanation; strong supporting details	Mostly clear explanation; good supporting details	Generally clear explanation; some supporting details	Explanation with few details and/or lack of focus	Explanation with lack of clarity and development
Organization/ Paragraphs	Uses paragraphs with clear structure and transitions	Paragraphs with logical structure; uses transitions	Attempts structured paragraphs; needs transitions	No paragraphs; structure not clear	No noticeable organization
Voice	Writer engaged; shows authority over subject	Writer generally engaged and authoritative	Writer involved with subject; shows some authority	Weak voice; little writer involvement	Writer not engaged with subject
Word Choice	Uses specific words for clarity and interest	Uses clear words and some vivid images	Words mostly clear; some interesting images	Vague, repetitive, or incorrect words	Incorrect or limited word choice
Sentences	Sentence structures appropriate, varied, interesting	Mostly well-crafted sentences; good variety	Correct sentences; some variety	Choppy sentences; no variety	Fragments or run-ons
Conventions	Excellent control and accuracy	Good control with few errors	Reasonable control; some errors	Many errors	Numerous errors

Rubric	4	3	2	1
Focus/Ideas	Clear, succinct explanation; strong supporting details	Fairly clear explanation; some good details	Explanation with few details and/or lack of focus	Explanation with lack of clarity and development
Organization/ Paragraphs	Uses paragraphs with clear structure and transitions	Paragraphs with logical structure; uses transitions	No paragraphs; structure not clear	No noticeable organization
Voice	Writer engaged; shows authority over subject	Writer engaged with subject	Weak voice; little writer involvement	Writer not engaged with subject
Word Choice	Specific, clear words	Some vivid images	Vague, repetitive, or incorrect words	Incorrect or limited word choice
Sentences	Sentence structures appropriate, varied, interesting	Fairly well-crafted sentences; some variety	Choppy sentences; no variety	Fragments or run-ons
Conventions	Excellent control	Reasonable control with few errors	Many errors	Numerous errors

18 Rubrics

Rubric	6	5	4	3	2	1
Focus/Ideas	Expository writing with clear thesis and strong details	Expository writing with plain thesis and good support	Expository writing with adequate thesis and support	Expository writing with vague thesis and little support	Expository writing with no thesis and/or weak support	Expository writing with no thesis or development
Organization/ Paragraphs	Logical thesis-body-conclusion structure	Clear structure for supporting details	Reasonable structure for details	Thesis or conclusion weak; details not organized	Lacks thesis and/or conclusion; no structure for details	Lacks organization and support
Voice	Authoritative, engaging, and individual	Engaged, pleasant; involved with subject	Sincere; generally involved with subject	Bland; not fully engaged	Little authority or attempt to deal with subject	Not involved with subject
Word Choice	Uses specific words to make strong case	Uses clear language to make persuasive argument	Some specific words to help make case	Some general or inexact words	Some vague, repetitive, or incorrect words	Incorrect or limited word choice
Sentences	Structures varied; smooth flow	Good variety; fluent sentences	Mostly fluent sentences; some variety	Mostly simple sentences; little variety	Choppy sentences; lacks variety	Fragments or run-ons
Conventions	Excellent control and accuracy	Good control with only minor errors	Reasonable control; few serious errors	Some serious errors	Many errors that distract	Numerous errors that disrupt meaning

Rubric	5	4	3	2	1
Focus/Ideas	Expository writing with clear thesis and strong details	Expository writing with plain thesis and good support	Expository writing with adequate thesis and support	Expository writing with vague thesis and little support	Expository writing with no thesis or development
Organization/ Paragraphs	Logical thesis-body-conclusion structure	Clear structure for supporting details	Reasonable structure for details	Lacks thesis or conclusion	Lacks organization and support
Voice	Authoritative, engaging, and individual	Engaged, pleasant; involved with subject	Sincere; generally involved with subject	Tries to deal with subject; has little authority	Not involved with subject
Word Choice	Uses specific words to make strong case	Uses clear language to make persuasive argument	Some specific words to help make case	Some vague, repetitive, or incorrect words	Incorrect or limited word choice
Sentences	Structures varied; smooth flow	Good variety; fluent sentences	Mostly fluent sentences; some variety	Choppy sentences; lacks variety	Fragments or run-ons
Conventions	Excellent control and accuracy	Good control with only minor errors	Reasonable control; few serious errors	Many errors that distract	Numerous errors that disrupt meaning

Rubric	4	3	2	1
Focus/Ideas	Expository writing with clear thesis and strong details	Expository writing with plain thesis and good support	Expository writing with vague thesis and little support	Expository writing with no thesis or development
Organization/ Paragraphs	Logical thesis-body-conclusion structure	Reasonable structure for supporting details	Lacks thesis or conclusion	Lacks organization and support
Voice	Authoritative, engaging, and individual	Somewhat involved with subject	Tries to deal with subject; has little authority	Not involved with subject
Word Choice	Uses specific words to make strong case	Argument persuasive; clear language	Some vague, repetitive, or incorrect words	Incorrect or limited word choice
Sentences	Structures varied; smooth flow	Control over most sentence structures	Choppy sentences; lacks variety	Fragments or run-ons
Conventions	Excellent control and accuracy	Reasonable control with few errors	Many errors	Numerous errors

Rubric	6	5	4	3	2	1
Focus/Ideas	Strong biographical study; only important details from life	Clear biographical study; mostly important details	Fairly clear biographical study; some important details	Biographical study with too many unimportant details	Biographical study with few details	Biographical study with no focus or development
Organization/ Paragraphs	Easy to follow; events in proper order	Events in logical order; easy to follow	Events in understandable order	Some events not in order	Events disorganized; hard to follow	Lacks organization
Voice	Knowledgeable, appropriate, and engaged	Appropriate for subject; mostly engaged	Mostly appropriate; generally engaged	Engaged at times; not always appropriate for subject	Tries to deal with subject but not fully engaged	Writer not involved with subject
Word Choice	Powerful verbs; strong descriptions	Clear language; some strong verbs	Mostly clear, strong language	Adequate language but lacking in color	Some vague, repetitive, or incorrect words	Incorrect or limited word choice
Sentences	Structures varied; clear and interesting	Variety good; mostly smooth	Adequate control of structures	Little variety; mostly simple sentences	Choppy sentences; lacks variety	Fragments or run-ons
Conventions	Excellent control and accuracy	Good control with only minor errors	Reasonable control; few serious errors	Some serious errors	Many errors that distract	Numerous errors that disrupt meaning

Rubric	5	4	3	2	1
Focus/Ideas	Strong biographical study; only important details from life	Clear biographical study; mostly important details	Biographical study fairly clear; some important details	Biographical study with few details	Biographical study with no focus or development
Organization/ Paragraphs	Easy to follow; events in proper order	Events in logical order; easy to follow	Events in understandable order	Events disorganized; hard to follow	Lacks organization
Voice	Knowledgeable, appropriate, and engaged	Appropriate for subject; mostly engaged	Mostly appropriate; generally engaged	Tries to deal with topic but not fully engaged	Writer not involved with subject
Word Choice	Powerful verbs; strong descriptions	Clear language; some strong verbs	Mostly clear, strong language	Some vague, repetitive, or incorrect words	Incorrect or limited word choice
Sentences	Structures varied; clear and interesting	Variety good; mostly smooth	Adequate control of structures	Choppy sentences; lacks variety	Fragments or run-ons
Conventions	Excellent control and accuracy	Good control with only minor errors	Reasonable control; few serious errors	Many errors that distract	Numerous errors that disrupt meaning

Rubric	4	3	2	1
Focus/Ideas	Clear biographical study; important details from life	Biographical study fairly clear; some good details	Biographical study with few details	Biographical study with no focus or development
Organization/ Paragraphs	Easy to follow; events in proper order	Events in reasonable order	Events somewhat disorganized	Lacks organization
Voice	Knowledgeable, appropriate	Appropriate for subject	Tries to deal with subject but not fully engaged	Writer not involved with subject
Word Choice	Powerful verbs; strong descriptions	Clear language; some strong verbs	Some vague, repetitive, or incorrect words	Incorrect or limited word choice
Sentences	Structures varied; clear and interesting	Variety good; mostly smooth	Choppy sentences; lacks variety	Fragments or run-ons
Conventions	Excellent control and accuracy	Reasonable control with few errors	Many errors	Numerous errors

Rubric	6	5	4	3	2	1
Focus/Ideas	Clear, focused rules	Rules clear; mostly on topic	Rules fairly clear; generally on topic	Rules unclear at times; sometimes off topic	Rules unclear: often stray from topic	Rules with no clarity or development
Organization/ Paragraphs	Clearly prioritized list; logical order	Good prioritization and order	Reasonable prioritization and order	Attempts to prioritize and order list	Unclear priorities; confusing	Lacks organization
Voice	Informed, straightforward; speaks directly to reader	Mostly informed; speaks to reader	Generally informed and direct	Sincere but not always engaged	Tries to deal with subject but not fully engaged	Writer not involved with subject
Word Choice	Uses specific words that stress importance	Uses clear language to explain rules	Reasonably clear language	Language too general	Some vague, repetitive, or incorrect words	Incorrect or limited word choice
Sentences	Structured for maximum understanding	Control over sentence structures	Some variety of sentences; mostly smooth	Little variety; simple structures	Choppy sentences; meandering	Run-ons; misuse of fragments
Conventions	Excellent control and accuracy	Good control with only minor errors	Reasonable control; few serious errors	Some serious errors	Many errors that distract	Numerous errors that disrupt meaning

Rubric	5	4	3	2	1
Focus/Ideas	Clear, focused rules	Rules clear; mostly on topic	Rules fairly clear; generally on topic	Rules unclear in places; stray from topic	Rules with no clarity or development
Organization/ Paragraphs	Clearly prioritized list; logical order	Good prioritization and order	Reasonable prioritization and order	Unclear priorities; confusing	Lacks organization
Voice	Informed, straightforward; speaks directly to reader	Mostly informed; speaks to reader	Generally informed and direct	Tries to deal with subject but not fully engaged	Writer not involved with subject
Word Choice	Uses specific words that stress importance	Uses clear language to explain rules	Reasonably clear language	Some vague, repetitive, or incorrect words	Incorrect or limited word choice
Sentences	Structured for maximum understanding	Control over sentence structures	Some variety of sentences; mostly smooth	Choppy sentences; meandering	Run-ons; misuse of fragments
Conventions	Excellent control and accuracy	Good control with only minor errors	Reasonable control; few serious errors	Many errors that distract	Numerous errors that disrupt meaning

Rubric	4	3	2	1
Focus/Ideas	Clear, focused rules	Rules fairly clear; mostly on topic	Rules unclear in places; stray from topic	Rules with no clarity or development
Organization/ Paragraphs	Clearly prioritized list; logical order	Reasonable prioritization and order	Unclear priorities; confusing	Lacks organization
Voice	Informed, straightforward; speaks directly to reader	Mostly informed; speaks to reader	Tries to deal with subject but not fully engaged	Writer not involved with subject
Word Choice	Uses specific words that stress importance	Uses clear language to explain rules	Some vague, repetitive, or incorrect words	Incorrect or limited word choice
Sentences	Structured for maximum understanding	Control over sentence structures	Choppy sentences; meandering	Run-ons; misuse of fragments
Conventions	Excellent control and accuracy	Reasonable control with few errors	Many errors	Numerous errors

Rubric	6	5	4	3	2	1
Focus/Ideas	Clear, focused e-mail; excellent support for opinion	E-mail clear; holds to purpose; good support for opinion	E-mail fairly clear; support for opinion	E-mail with stated purpose and some support for opinion	E-mail that strays from purpose; lacks support	E-mail that lacks clarity and development
Organization/ Paragraphs	Uses logical organization and smooth transitions	Mostly logical organization; some smooth transitions	Organization fairly logical; some transitions	Lapses in organization; needs transitions	Lacks flow	Lacks organization and support
Voice	Sincere, direct, engaging	Sincere; mostly direct and engaging	Sincere and generally engaging	Sincere but not direct or engaging	Tries to deal with subject but not fully engaged	Not involved with subject
Word Choice	Uses words appropriate for audience	Mostly uses words appropriate for audience	Words generally suitable for audience	Some words unsuitable for audience	Some vague or inappropriate words	Incorrect or limited word choice
Sentences	Varied, well-constructed sentences	Correctly constructed sentences; good variety	Sentences mostly correct; some variety	Mostly simple sentences; little variety	Choppy sentences; no variety	Unclear sentences
Conventions	Excellent control and accuracy	Good control with only minor errors	Reasonable control; few serious errors	Some serious errors	Many errors that distract	Numerous errors that disrupt meaning

Rubric	5	4	3	2	1
Focus/Ideas	Clear, focused e-mail; excellent support for opinion	E-mail clear; holds to purpose; good support for opinion	E-mail fairly clear; support for opinion	E-mail that strays from purpose; lacks support	E-mail that lacks clarity and development
Organization/ Paragraphs	Uses logical organization and smooth transitions	Mostly logical organization; some smooth transitions	Organization fairly logical; some transitions	Lacks flow	Lacks organization and support
Voice	Sincere, direct, engaging	Sincere; mostly direct and engaging	Sincere and generally engaging	Tries to deal with subject but not fully engaged	Not involved with subject
Word Choice	Uses words appropriate for audience	Mostly uses words appropriate for audience	Words generally suitable for audience	Some vague or inappropriate words	Incorrect or limited word choice
Sentences	Varied, well-constructed sentences	Correctly constructed sentences; good variety	Sentences mostly correct; some variety	Choppy sentences; little variety	Unclear sentences
Conventions	Excellent control and accuracy	Good control with only minor errors	Reasonable control; few serious errors	Many errors that distract	Numerous errors that disrupt meaning

Rubric	4	3	2	1
Focus/Ideas	Clear, focused e-mail; excellent support for opinion	E-mail fairly clear; holds to purpose; adequate support	E-mail that strays from purpose; lacks support	E-mail that lacks clarity and development
Organization/ Paragraphs	Uses logical organization and transitions	Uses reasonably logical organization	Lacks flow	Lacks organization and support
Voice	Sincere, direct, engaging	Sincere and generally engaging	Tries to deal with subject but not fully engaged	Not involved with subject
Word Choice	Uses words appropriate for audience	Mostly uses words appropriate for audience	Some vague or inappropriate words	Incorrect or limited word choice
Sentences	Varied sentences	Some variety	Choppy sentences; little variety	Unclear sentences
Conventions	Excellent control and accuracy	Reasonable control with few errors	Many errors	Numerous errors

Rubric	6	5	4	3	2	1
Focus/Ideas	Strong, focused paragraph; many vivid details	Clear paragraph; good details	Generally focused paragraph; adequate details	Paragraph off topic at times; needs more details	Paragraph with few details and/or lack of focus	Paragraph lacking clarity and development
Organization/ Paragraphs	Clear, logical compare/contrast structure	Logical compare/contrast structure	Organized compare/contrast structure	Misplaced details in compare/contrast structure	Structure not clear	Lacks organization
Voice	Engaging, lively; shows authority	Mostly engaging and authoritative	Sincere voice; shows some authority	Uncertain voice; engaged at times	Little sense of writer	Writer not engaged with subject
Word Choice	Uses transition words and specific words effectively	Uses transition words and specific words well	Some transitions; some specific words	Adequate but general words; few transitions	Vague, repetitive or incorrect words; few transitions	Incorrect or limited word choice
Sentences	Sentence structures varied, interesting	Well-constructed sentences; some variety	Correct sentences; some variety	Too many simple sentences; little variety	Choppy sentences; no variety	Fragments or run-ons
Conventions	Excellent control and accuracy	Good control with only minor errors	Reasonable control; few serious errors	Some serious errors	Many errors that distract	Numerous errors that disrupt meaning

Rubric	5	4	3	2	1
Focus/Ideas	Strong, focused paragraph; many vivid details	Clear paragraph; good details	Generally focused paragraph; adequate details	Paragraph with few details and/or lack of focus	Paragraph lacking clarity and development
Organization/ Paragraphs	Clear, logical compare/contrast structure	Logical compare/contrast structure	Organized compare/contrast structure	Structure not clear	Lacks organization
Voice	Engaging, lively; shows authority	Mostly engaging and authoritative	Sincere voice; shows some authority	Little sense of writer	Writer not engaged with subject
Word Choice	Uses transition words and specific words effectively	Uses transition words and specific words well	Some transitions; some specific words	Vague, repetitive or incorrect words; few transitions	Incorrect or limited word choice
Sentences	Sentence structures varied, interesting	Well-constructed sentences; some variety	Correct sentences; some variety	Choppy sentences; little variety	Fragments or run-ons
Conventions	Excellent control and accuracy	Good control with only minor errors	Reasonable control; few serious errors	Many errors that distract	Numerous errors that disrupt meaning

Rubric	4	3	2	1
Focus/Ideas	Strong, focused paragraph; many vivid details	Clear paragraph; good details	Paragraph with few details and/or lack of focus	Paragraph lacking clarity and development
Organization/ Paragraphs	Clear, logical compare/contrast structure	Logical structure	Structure not clear	Lacks organization
Voice	Engaging, lively; shows authority	Writer fully engaged with subject	Little sense of writer	Writer not engaged with subject
Word Choice	Uses transition words and specific words	Some transitions; some specific words	Vague, repetitive or incorrect words; few transitions	Incorrect or limited word choice
Sentences	Sentence structures varied, interesting	Control over simple sentence structures	Choppy sentences; little variety	Fragments or run-ons
Conventions	Excellent control and accuracy	Reasonable control with few errors	Many errors	Numerous errors

Rubric (6-point)

Rubric	6	5	4	3	2	1
Focus/Ideas	Focused news story with complete coverage of event	Focused news story; answers 5 Ws and How	Mostly focused news story; answers most Ws and How	News story focused at times; one or two Ws missing	Poorly focused news story; many unanswered questions	News story lacking clarity and development
Organization/ Paragraphs	Strong lead sentence; then prioritized details	Good lead sentence; then details mostly prioritized	Adequate lead sentence; some prioritized details	Weak lead sentence; few prioritized details	Unclear priorities; no lead sentence	Lacks organization
Voice	Authoritative, engaged, objective	Shows authority on subject	Writer mostly objective, with some authority	Writer not fully engaged or objective	Subjective or not authoritative	Not involved with subject or not factual
Word Choice	Specific words; communicates clearly	Clear language	Mostly clear language	Words correct but often too general	Some vague, repetitive, or incorrect words	Incorrect or limited word choice
Sentences	Structured simply for quick reading; smooth flow	Clear sentences; good flow	Generally clear, smooth sentences	Simple sentences; not very smooth	Choppy sentences; meandering	Fragments, run-on sentences
Conventions	Excellent control and accuracy	Good control with only minor errors	Reasonable control; some errors	Some confusing errors	Errors that may prevent understanding	Frequent errors that affect meaning

Rubric (5-point)

Rubric	5	4	3	2	1
Focus/Ideas	Focused news story with complete coverage of event	Focused news story; answers 5 Ws and how	Mostly focused news story; answers most Ws and how	Some Ws missing in news story	News story lacking clarity and development
Organization/ Paragraphs	Strong lead sentence; then prioritized details	Good lead sentence; then details mostly prioritized	Adequate lead sentence; some prioritized details	Unclear priorities; no lead sentence	Lacks organization
Voice	Authoritative, engaged, objective	Shows authority on subject	Writer mostly objective, with some authority	Subjective or not authoritative	Not involved with subject or not factual
Word Choice	Specific words; communicates clearly	Clear language	Mostly clear language	Some vague, repetitive, or incorrect words	Incorrect or limited word choice
Sentences	Structured simply for quick reading; smooth flow	Clear sentences; good flow	Generally clear, smooth sentences	Choppy sentences; meandering	Fragments, run-on sentences
Conventions	Excellent control and accuracy	Good control with only minor errors	Reasonable control; some errors	Errors that may prevent understanding	Frequent errors that affect meaning

Rubric (4-point)

Rubric	4	3	2	1
Focus/Ideas	Focused news story with complete coverage of event	News story that answers 5 Ws and how	Some Ws missing in news story	News story lacking clarity and development
Organization/ Paragraphs	Strong lead sentence; prioritized information	Good lead sentence; reasonable prioritization	No lead sentence; unclear priorities	Lacks organization
Voice	Authoritative, engaged, objective	Shows authority on subject	Subjective or not authoritative	Not involved with subject
Word Choice	Specific words; communicates clearly	Clear language	Some vague, repetitive, or incorrect words	Incorrect or limited word choice
Sentences	Structured simply for quick reading	Control over sentence structure	Choppy sentences; meandering	Fragments, run-on sentences
Conventions	Excellent control and accuracy	Reasonable control with few errors	Errors that may prevent understanding	Frequent errors that affect meaning

Rubric	6	5	4	3	2	1
Focus/Ideas	Story with quality details; strong plot	Story with good details; clear plot	Story with adequate details and plot	Story with gaps in plot; needs more details	Story unfocused; little plot	Story lacking clarity and development
Organization/ Paragraphs	Exciting beginning, middle; strong end	Good beginning, middle, and end	Recognizable beginning, middle, and end	Weak beginning or end; gaps in middle	Disorganized at times; missing beginning or end	Lacks organization
Voice	Shows personality; creates distinct mood; interactive	Engaged, interested writer; creates mood	Generally caring writer; some interaction and mood	Somewhat involved with subject; little mood	Weak; lacks personality and mood	Not involved with subject; no mood created
Word Choice	Vivid, intriguing words; natural dialogue	Clear, interesting language; use of dialogue	Some vivid words; some dialogue	Few vivid words; attempt at dialogue	Some vague or repetitive words; little dialogue	Limited word choice; no dialogue
Sentences	Varied, smoothly connected sentences	Good variety; control of structures	Correct sentences; some variety	Mostly correct sentences; overly simple	Choppy sentences; lacks variety	Fragments, run-on sentences
Conventions	Excellent control and accuracy	Good control with only minor errors	Reasonable control; some errors	Some confusing errors	Errors that may prevent understanding	Frequent errors that affect meaning

Rubric	5	4	3	2	1
Focus/Ideas	Story with quality details; strong plot	Story with good details; clear plot	Story with adequate details and plot	Story unfocused; little plot	Story lacking clarity and development
Organization/ Paragraphs	Exciting beginning, middle; strong end	Good beginning, middle, and end	Recognizable beginning, middle, and end	Disorganized at times; missing beginning or end	Lacks organization
Voice	Shows personality; creates distinct mood; interactive	Engaged, interested writer; creates mood	Generally caring writer; some interaction and mood	Somewhat involved with subject; little mood	Not involved with subject; no mood created
Word Choice	Vivid, intriguing words; natural dialogue	Clear, interesting language; use of dialogue	Some precise nouns, verbs, adjectives; some dialogue	Some vague or repetitive words; little dialogue	Limited word choice; no dialogue
Sentences	Varied, smoothly connected sentences	Good variety, control of structures	Correct sentences; some variety	Choppy sentences; lacks variety	Fragments, run-on sentences
Conventions	Excellent control and accuracy	Good control with only minor errors	Reasonable control; some errors	Errors that may prevent understanding	Frequent errors that affect meaning

Rubric	4	3	2	1
Focus/Ideas	Story with quality details; strong plot	Story with good details; clear plot	Story unfocused at times; little plot	Story lacking clarity and development
Organization/ Paragraphs	Exciting beginning, middle; strong end	Recognizable beginning, middle, and end	Disorganized at times; missing beginning or end	Lacks organization
Voice	Shows personality; creates mood; interactive	Engaged, mostly interested writer; some mood	Somewhat involved with subject; little mood	Not involved with subject; no mood created
Word Choice	Vivid, intriguing words; natural dialogue	Clear, interesting language; use of dialogue	Some vague or repetitive words; little dialogue	Limited word choice; no dialogue
Sentences	Structures varied; smooth flow	Control over simple sentence structures	Choppy sentences; lacks variety	Fragments, run-on sentences
Conventions	Excellent control and accuracy	Reasonable control with few errors	Errors that may prevent understanding	Frequent errors that affect meaning

Rubric (6-point)

Rubric	6	5	4	3	2	1
Focus/Ideas	Description with vivid details that highlight time and place	Description with good details of time and place	Description with some good details of time and place	Description that could use more details of time and place	Nonspecific description of setting	No description of setting
Organization/ Paragraphs	Details ordered spatially or by importance	Order mostly by spatial features or importance	Some use of spatial order or order of importance	Little use of spatial order or order of importance	Confused order of details	No discernible order
Voice	Engaging, lively, knowledgeable voice	Writer fully involved with subject	Voice interesting, lively at times	Writer sincere but not fully engaged	Somewhat involved with subject	Not involved with subject
Word Choice	Setting conveyed through specific words, vivid images	Setting portrayed through clear language	Setting conveyed through generally clear language	Needs more specific words and vivid images	Some vague or repetitive words; little detail	Limited, dull word choice
Sentences	Structures varied; mature writing style	Good control over sentence structures	Reasonable control over sentence structures	Mostly simple structures; few errors; little variety	Short, choppy sentences; lacks variety; some errors	Fragments, run-on sentences
Conventions	Excellent control and accuracy	Good control with only minor errors	Reasonable control; some errors	Some confusing errors	Errors that may prevent understanding	Frequent errors that affect meaning

Rubric (5-point)

Rubric	5	4	3	2	1
Focus/Ideas	Description with vivid details that highlight time and place	Description with good details of time and place	Description with some good details of time and place	Nonspecific description of setting	No description of setting
Organization/ Paragraphs	Details ordered spatially or by importance	Order mostly by spatial features or importance	Some use of spatial order or order of importance	Confused order of details	No discernible order
Voice	Engaging, lively, knowledgeable voice	Writer fully involved with subject	Voice interesting, lively at times	Somewhat involved with subject	Not involved with subject
Word Choice	Setting conveyed through specific words, vivid images	Setting portrayed through clear language	Setting portrayed through mostly clear language	Some vague or repetitive words; little detail	Limited word choice
Sentences	Structures varied; mature writing style	Good control over sentence structures	Reasonable control over sentence structures	Short, choppy, simple sentences; lacks variety	Fragments, run-on sentences
Conventions	Excellent control and accuracy	Good control with only minor errors	Reasonable control; some errors	Errors that may prevent understanding	Frequent errors that affect meaning

Rubric (4-point)

Rubric	4	3	2	1
Focus/Ideas	Description with vivid details that highlight time and place	Description with good details of time and place	Nonspecific description of setting	No description of setting
Organization/ Paragraphs	Details ordered spatially or by importance	Order mostly by spatial features or importance	Confused order of details	No discernible order
Voice	Engaging, lively, knowledgeable voice	Writer involved with subject	Somewhat involved with subject	Not involved with subject
Word Choice	Setting conveyed through specific words, vivid images	Setting portrayed through clear language	Some vague or repetitive words; little detail	Limited word choice
Sentences	Structures varied; mature writing style	Control over sentence structures	Short, choppy, simple sentences; lacks variety	Fragments, run-on sentences
Conventions	Excellent control and accuracy	Reasonable control with few errors	Errors that may prevent understanding	Frequent errors that affect meaning

Rubric	6	5	4	3	2	1
Focus/Ideas	Script with strong, natural dialogue and clear action	Script with good dialogue and action	Script with mostly believable dialogue and action	Script with sometimes unnatural dialogue or weak action	Script with weak or unnatural dialogue and action	Script with little or no dialogue or action
Organization/ Paragraphs	Events told in sequence; uses script format effectively	Events in logical order; script format correct	Events in mostly logical order; script format correct	Some events out of order; uncertain use of script format	Sequence and script format attempted	Lacks sequence of events or script format
Voice	Engaging, lively; well-defined characters	Entertaining; differentiates characters	Mostly engaging; interesting characters	Some involvement with characters	Tries to be involved with characters	Not involved with characters
Word Choice	Specific words, vivid images	Clear, interesting language	Generally clear language; some vivid images	Words more often general than specific	Some vague, repetitive, or incorrect words	Incorrect or limited word choice
Sentences	Sentences well constructed and varied; sounds like speech	Control over sentence structures; sounds like speech	Correct sentences; some variety; resembles speech	Simple structures often lacking variety or naturalness	Choppy sentences; lacks variety	Run-on sentences, inappropriate fragments
Conventions	Excellent control and accuracy	Good control with only minor errors	Reasonable control; some errors	Some confusing errors	Errors that may prevent understanding	Frequent errors that affect meaning

Rubric	5	4	3	2	1
Focus/Ideas	Script with strong, natural dialogue and clear action	Script with good dialogue and action	Script with mostly believable dialogue and action	Script with weak or unnatural dialogue and action	Script with little or no dialogue or action
Organization/ Paragraphs	Events told in sequence; uses script format effectively	Events in logical order; script format correct	Events in mostly logical order; script format correct	Sequence and script format attempted	Lacks sequence of events or script format
Voice	Engaging, lively; well-defined characters	Entertaining; differentiates characters	Mostly engaging; interesting characters	Tries to be involved with characters	Not involved with characters
Word Choice	Specific words, vivid images	Clear, interesting language	Generally clear language; some vivid images	Some vague, repetitive, or incorrect words	Incorrect or limited word choice
Sentences	Sentences well constructed and varied; sounds like speech	Control over sentence structures; sounds like speech	Correct sentences; some variety; resembles speech	Choppy sentences; lacks variety	Run-on sentences, inappropriate fragments
Conventions	Excellent control and accuracy	Good control with only minor errors	Reasonable control; some errors	Errors that may prevent understanding	Frequent errors that affect meaning

Rubric	4	3	2	1
Focus/Ideas	Script with strong, natural dialogue and clear action	Script with good dialogue and action	Script with weak or unnatural dialogue and action	Script with little or no dialogue or action
Organization/ Paragraphs	Events told in sequence; uses correct script format	Events in logical order; script format mostly correct	Sequence and script format attempted	Lacks sequence of events or script format
Voice	Engaging, lively; well-defined characters	Characters differentiated from one another	Tries to be involved with characters	Not involved with characters
Word Choice	Specific words, vivid images	Clear, interesting language	Some vague, repetitive, or incorrect words	Incorrect or limited word choice
Sentences	Sentences well constructed and varied	Control over sentence structures	Choppy sentences; lacks variety	Run-on sentences, inappropriate fragments
Conventions	Excellent control and accuracy	Reasonable control with few errors	Errors that may prevent understanding	Frequent errors that affect meaning

Rubric	6	5	4	3	2	1
Focus/Ideas	Clear, focused summary; holds reader's attention	Clear summary; good details	Reasonably clear summary; some good details	Somewhat unfocused summary; needs more details	Few details and/or lack of focus in summary	Summary lacking in details or development
Organization/ Paragraphs	Excellent topic sentence; logical, smooth order	Good topic sentence and logical structure	Has topic sentence and mostly logical structure	Weak topic sentence; recognizable structure	Structure not clear; unfocused topic sentence	Lacks structure and topic sentence
Voice	Engaging, lively; shows authority	Writer engaged with subject; shows authority	Generally engaging; some authority	Sincere voice with little authority	Weak voice; lacks authority	Not engaged with subject
Word Choice	Thorough knowledge of subject; uses specific words	Good sense of subject; uses mostly specific words	Some knowledge of subject; uses some specific words	Sense of subject; uses adequate but general words	Uses some vague, repetitive, or incorrect words	Incorrect, limited word choice
Sentences	Sentence structures varied and interesting	Good control over sentence structures	Adequate control over sentence structures	Mostly correct but simple structures	Choppy sentences; no variety; some errors	Fragments, run-on sentences
Conventions	Excellent control and accuracy	Good control with only minor errors	Reasonable control; some errors	Some confusing errors	Errors that may prevent understanding	Frequent errors that affect meaning

Rubric	5	4	3	2	1
Focus/Ideas	Clear, focused summary; holds reader's attention	Clear summary; good details	Reasonably clear summary; some good details	Few details and/or lack of focus in summary	Summary lacking in details or development
Organization/ Paragraphs	Excellent topic sentence; logical, smooth order	Good topic sentence and logical structure	Has topic sentence and mostly logical structure	Structure not clear; unfocused topic sentence	Lacks structure and topic sentence
Voice	Engaging, lively; shows authority	Writer engaged with subject; shows authority	Generally engaging; some authority	Weak voice	Not engaged with subject
Word Choice	Thorough knowledge of subject; uses specific words	Good sense of subject; uses mostly specific words	Some knowledge of subject; uses some specific words	Uses some vague, repetitive, or incorrect words	Incorrect, limited word choice
Sentences	Sentence structures varied and interesting	Good control over sentence structures	Adequate control over sentence structures	Choppy sentences; no variety	Fragments, run-on sentences
Conventions	Excellent control and accuracy	Good control with only minor errors	Reasonable control; some errors	Errors that may prevent understanding	Frequent errors that affect meaning

Rubric	4	3	2	1
Focus/Ideas	Clear, focused summary; holds reader's attention	Clear summary; good details	Few details and/or lack of focus in summary	Summary lacking in details or development
Organization/ Paragraphs	Excellent topic sentence; logical, smooth order	Uses topic sentence and logical structure	Structure not clear; unfocused topic sentence	Lacks structure and topic sentence
Voice	Engaging, lively; shows authority	Writer engaged with subject	Weak voice	Not engaged with subject
Word Choice	Thorough knowledge of subject; uses specific words	Good sense of subject; uses mostly specific words	Uses some vague, repetitive, or incorrect words	Incorrect, limited word choice
Sentences	Sentence structures varied and interesting	Control over sentence structures	Choppy sentences; no variety	Fragments, run-on sentences
Conventions	Excellent control and accuracy	Reasonable control with few errors	Errors that may prevent understanding	Frequent errors that affect meaning

Rubric	6	5	4	3	2	1
Focus/Ideas	Review supporting opinion with strong details	Review with clear opinion and good supporting details	Review with stated opinion; some good supporting details	Review with unclear opinion; some supporting details	Review missing either opinion or sufficient details	Review lacking clarity or development
Organization/ Paragraphs	Introduction; main ideas followed by details; conclusion	Has all parts; main ideas/details arranged logically	Has all parts; main ideas/details in reasonable order	Missing one part; main ideas/details not well organized	Tends to stray; lacks introduction and conclusion	Lacks organization
Voice	Engaging, lively, individual	Interested and interesting	Pleasant; generally involved	Sincere but not engaging or individual	Tries to be involved with subject	Not involved with subject
Word Choice	Specific words, vivid images	Clear, interesting language	Generally clear language; some vivid images	Words more often general than specific	Some vague, repetitive, or incorrect words	Incorrect or limited word choice
Sentences	Structures well crafted, varied; sustains interest	Well-written sentences; good variety	Correct sentences; some variety	Mostly correct sentences; little variety	Choppy sentences; lacks variety	Fragments, run-on sentences
Conventions	Excellent control and accuracy	Good control with minor errors	Reasonable control; some errors	Some serious errors	Errors that may prevent understanding	Frequent errors that affect meaning

Rubric	5	4	3	2	1
Focus/Ideas	Review supporting opinion with strong details	Review with clear opinion and good supporting details	Review with stated opinion; some good supporting details	Review with unclear opinion and some supporting details	Review lacking clarity or development
Organization/ Paragraphs	Introduction; main ideas followed by details; conclusion	Has all parts; order of ideas/details mostly logical	Has all parts; main ideas/details in reasonable order	Tends to stray; lacks introduction and conclusion	Lacks organization
Voice	Engaging, lively individual	Interested and interesting	Pleasant; generally involved	Tries to be involved with subject	Not involved with subject
Word Choice	Specific words, vivid images	Clear, interesting language	Generally clear language; some vivid images	Some vague, repetitive, or incorrect words	Incorrect or limited word choice
Sentences	Structures well crafted, varied; sustains interest	Well-written sentences; good variety	Correct sentences; some variety	Choppy sentences; lacks variety	Fragments, run-on sentences
Conventions	Excellent control and accuracy	Good control with only minor errors	Reasonable control; some errors	Errors that may prevent understanding	Frequent errors that affect meaning

Rubric	4	3	2	1
Focus/Ideas	Review supporting opinion with strong details	Review with clear opinion and good supporting details	Review with unclear opinion and few supporting details	Review lacking clarity or development
Organization/ Paragraphs	Introduction; main ideas followed by details; conclusion	Has all parts; order of ideas/details mostly logical	Tends to stray; lacks introduction and conclusion	Lacks organization
Voice	Engaging, lively, individual	Writer involved with subject	Tries to be involved with subject	Not involved with subject
Word Choice	Specific words, vivid images	Clear, interesting language	Some vague, repetitive, or incorrect words	Incorrect or limited word choice
Sentences	Structures varied; sustains interest	Control over simple sentence structures	Choppy sentences; lacks variety	Fragments, run-on sentences
Conventions	Excellent control and accuracy	Reasonable control with few errors	Errors that may prevent understanding	Frequent errors that affect meaning

Rubrics 29

Rubric	6	5	4	3	2	1
Focus/Ideas	Letter with strong supporting details; focused argument	Letter with good details; focused argument	Letter with some good support; reasonable argument	Letter with some supporting details; weak argument	Letter with few supporting details; unclear argument	Letter with no argument or development
Organization/ Paragraphs	Logical order; argument followed by detailed support	Order mostly logical; main idea, then details	Argument first, then details in generally logical order	Misplaced argument; somewhat disorganized details	Tends to stray; many details not in order	Lacks organization
Voice	Formal, persuasive, individual	Persuasive; involved with subject	Mostly persuasive and involved with subject	Somewhat persuasive but not fully involved	Tries to be involved with subject	Not involved with subject
Word Choice	Specific, persuasive words	Clear, mostly persuasive words	Generally clear, persuasive words	Few specific or persuasive words	Some vague, repetitive, or incorrect words	Incorrect or limited word choice
Sentences	Structures clear and varied; smooth progression	Good control over sentence structures	Correct sentence structures; some variety	Overly simple; little variety	Choppy sentences; lacks variety	Fragments, run-on sentences
Conventions	Excellent control and accuracy	Good control with only minor errors	Reasonable control; some errors	Some serious errors	Errors that may prevent understanding	Frequent errors that affect meaning

Rubric	5	4	3	2	1
Focus/Ideas	Letter with strong supporting details; focused argument	Letter with good details; focused argument	Letter with reasonable argument, some support	Letter with few supporting details; unclear argument	Letter with no argument or development
Organization/ Paragraphs	Logical order; argument followed by detailed support	Order mostly logical; main idea, then details	Argument first, then details in generally logical order	Tends to stray; some details not in order	Lacks organization
Voice	Formal, persuasive, individual	Persuasive; involved with subject	Mostly persuasive and involved with subject	Tries to be involved with subject	Not involved with subject
Word Choice	Specific, persuasive words	Clear, mostly persuasive words	Generally clear, persuasive words	Some vague, repetitive, or incorrect words	Incorrect or limited word choice
Sentences	Structures clear and varied; smooth progression	Good control over sentence structures	Correct sentence structures; some variety	Choppy sentences; lacks variety	Fragments, run-on sentences
Conventions	Excellent control and accuracy	Good control with only minor errors	Reasonable control; some errors	Errors that may prevent understanding	Frequent errors that affect meaning

Rubric	4	3	2	1
Focus/Ideas	Letter with strong supporting details; focused argument	Letter with good details; reasonably focused argument	Letter with few supporting details; unclear argument	Letter with no argument or development
Organization/ Paragraphs	Logical order; argument followed by detailed support	Order mostly logical; main idea, then details	Tends to stray; some details not in order	Lacks organization
Voice	Formal, persuasive, individual	Writer involved with subject	Tries to be involved with subject	Not involved with subject
Word Choice	Specific, persuasive words	Clear, mostly persuasive words	Some vague, repetitive, or incorrect words	Incorrect or limited word choice
Sentences	Structures clear and varied	Control over simple sentence structures	Choppy sentences; lacks variety	Fragments, run-on sentences
Conventions	Excellent control and accuracy	Reasonable control with few errors	Errors that may prevent understanding	Frequent errors that affect meaning

Rubric	6	5	4	3	2	1
Focus/Ideas	Poem with strong emphasis on theme; clear imagery	Poem with good focus on theme; good imagery	Poem reasonably focused with some clear images	Poem with uneven focus on theme; few images	Little follow-through on theme in poem	Poem lacking clarity or development
Organization/Paragraphs	Creative, fitting structure; startling image sequence	Takes risks in structure and sequence	Interesting structure; images in recognizable sequence	Little grasp of poetic structure; images not ordered	Tends toward monotony	Lacks organization
Voice	Engaging, individual presence	Writer present in poem	Some sense of writer in poem	Little sense of poet	Tries to be present; not successful	Not present in poem
Word Choice	Vivid, unusual words; striking figures of speech	Clear, interesting words; vivid figures of speech	Clear words; some figures of speech	Adequate language; needs figures of speech	Some vague, repetitive, or incorrect words	Incorrect or limited word choice
Sentences	Effective sentences or purposeful fragments	Clear sentences or fragments	Conscious arrangement of sentences or fragments	Mix of words, fragments, sentences	Ineffective arrangement of words	Confusing sentences or word arrangement
Conventions	Excellent control and accuracy	Good control with only minor errors	Reasonable control; some errors	Some serious errors	Errors that may prevent understanding	Frequent errors that affect meaning

Rubric	5	4	3	2	1
Focus/Ideas	Poem with strong emphasis on theme; clear imagery	Poem with good focus on theme; good imagery	Poem reasonably focused with some clear images	Little follow-through on theme in poem	Poem lacking clarity or development
Organization/Paragraphs	Creative, fitting structure; startling image sequence	Takes risks in structure and sequence	Interesting structure; images in recognizable sequence	Tends toward monotony	Lacks organization
Voice	Engaging, individual presence	Writer present in poem	Some sense of writer in poem	Tries to be present; not successful	Not present in poem
Word Choice	Vivid, unusual words; striking figures of speech	Clear, interesting words; vivid figures of speech	Clear words; some figures of speech	Some vague, repetitive, or incorrect words	Incorrect or limited word choice
Sentences	Effective sentences or purposeful fragments	Clear sentences or fragments	Conscious arrangement of sentences or fragments	Ineffective arrangement of words	Confusing sentences or word arrangement
Conventions	Excellent control and accuracy	Good control with only minor errors	Reasonable control; some errors	Errors that may prevent understanding	Frequent errors that affect meaning

Rubric	4	3	2	1
Focus/Ideas	Poem with strong emphasis on theme; clear imagery	Poem reasonably focused and clear	Little follow-through on theme in poem	Poem lacking clarity or development
Organization/Paragraphs	Creative, fitting structure; startling image sequence	Takes risks in structure and sequence	Tends toward monotony	Lacks organization
Voice	Engaging, individual presence	Writer present in poem	Tries to be present	Not present in poem
Word Choice	Specific, unusual words and language	Clear, interesting words and language	Some vague, repetitive, or incorrect words	Incorrect or limited word choice
Sentences	Effective sentences or purposeful fragments	Clear sentences or fragments	Ineffective arrangement of words	Confusing sentences or word arrangement
Conventions	Excellent control and accuracy	Reasonable control with few errors	Errors that may prevent understanding	Frequent errors that affect meaning

Rubric	6	5	4	3	2	1
Focus/Ideas	Brochure with clear focus; strong supporting details	Brochure mostly focused; good details	Brochure generally focused; some good details	Brochure off topic at times; some details	Brochure with unclear focus; few supporting details	Brochure lacking clarity or development
Organization/ Paragraphs	Logical order; "bite-size" chunks for convenience	Order mostly logical; mostly compact text	Generally logical order and focused text	Order sometimes confused; needs more paragraphs	Tends to stray; lengthy paragraphs	Lacks organization
Voice	Engaging, lively, knowledgeable	Mostly knowledgeable, engaging	Shows some involvement and knowledge	Engaged at times but lacking in knowledge	Tries to be involved with subject	Not involved with subject
Word Choice	Specific words to promote and inform	Clear, interesting language; mostly informative	Clear language; somewhat informative	General language; not very informative	Some vague, repetitive, or incorrect words	Incorrect or limited word choice
Sentences	Structures varied; creates and sustains interest	Good control of various sentence structures	Correct sentences; some variety	Mostly simple sentences; little variety	Choppy sentences; lacks variety	Fragments, run-on sentences
Conventions	Excellent control and accuracy	Good control with only minor errors	Reasonable control; some errors	Some serious errors	Errors that may prevent understanding	Frequent errors that affect meaning

Rubric	5	4	3	2	1
Focus/Ideas	Brochure with clear focus; strong supporting details	Brochure mostly focused; good details	Brochure with some focus, adequate details	Brochure with unclear focus; few supporting details	Brochure lacking clarity or development
Organization/ Paragraphs	Logical order; "bite-size" chunks for convenience	Order mostly logical; mostly compact text	Generally logical order and focused text	Tends to stray; lengthy paragraphs	Lacks organization
Voice	Engaging, lively, knowledgeable	Mostly knowledgeable, engaging	Shows some involvement and knowledge	Tries to be involved with subject	Not involved with subject
Word Choice	Specific words to promote and inform	Clear, interesting language; mostly informative	Clear language; somewhat informative	Some vague, repetitive, or incorrect words	Incorrect or limited word choice
Sentences	Structures varied; creates and sustains interest	Good control of various sentence structures	Correct sentences; some variety	Choppy sentences; lacks variety	Fragments, run-on sentences
Conventions	Excellent control and accuracy	Good control with only minor errors	Reasonable control; some errors	Errors that may prevent understanding	Frequent errors that affect meaning

Rubric	4	3	2	1
Focus/Ideas	Brochure with clear focus; strong supporting details	Brochure reasonably focused; good details	Brochure with unclear focus; few supporting details	Brochure lacking clarity or development
Organization/ Paragraphs	Logical order; "bite-size" chunks for convenience	Order mostly logical; mostly compact text	Tends to stray; lengthy paragraphs	Lacks organization
Voice	Engaging, lively, knowledgeable	Writer involved with subject	Tries to be involved with subject	Not involved with subject
Word Choice	Specific words to promote and inform	Clear, interesting language; fairly informative	Some vague, repetitive, or incorrect words	Incorrect or limited word choice
Sentences	Structures varied; creates and sustains interest	Control over simple sentence structures	Choppy sentences; lacks variety	Fragments, run-on sentences
Conventions	Excellent control and accuracy	Reasonable control with few errors	Errors that may prevent understanding	Frequent errors that affect meaning

Rubric	6	5	4	3	2	1
Focus/Ideas	Clear, focused ad that motivates reader	Clear, interesting ad	Generally clear, focused ad	Ad with unclear focus and some details	Ad with few details and/or lack of focus	Ad lacking clarity and development
Organization/ Paragraphs	Logical, creative, easy to follow	Logical, interesting structure	Logical structure; mostly easy to follow	Scattered; hard to follow	Structure not clear	Lacks organization
Voice	Engaging, provocative, persuasive	Enthusiasm about subject evident	Shows some enthusiasm for subject	Sincere but not very persuasive	Weak voice	No enthusiasm or interest evident
Word Choice	Specific, persuasive words; dynamic copy	Good sense of writing to persuade	Some specific words; generally persuasive	Too many general words to be persuasive	Some vague, repetitive, or incorrect words	Incorrect, limited word choice
Sentences	Sentence structures varied, creative	Some creative structures; good variety	Generally interesting sentences; some variety	Little variety or creativity	Choppy sentences; no variety	Fragments, run-on sentences
Conventions	Excellent control and accuracy	Good control with only minor errors	Reasonable control; some errors	Some serious errors	Errors that may prevent understanding	Frequent errors that affect meaning

Rubric	5	4	3	2	1
Focus/Ideas	Clear, focused ad that motivates reader	Clear, interesting ad	Generally clear, focused ad	Ad with few details and/or lack of focus	Ad lacking clarity and development
Organization/ Paragraphs	Logical, creative, easy to follow	Logical, interesting structure	Logical structure; mostly easy to follow	Structure not clear	Lacks organization
Voice	Engaging, provocative, persuasive	Enthusiasm about subject evident	Shows some enthusiasm for subject	Weak voice	No enthusiasm or interest evident
Word Choice	Specific, persuasive words; dynamic copy	Good sense of writing to persuade	Some specific words; generally persuasive	Some vague, repetitive, or incorrect words	Incorrect, limited word choice
Sentences	Sentence structures varied, creative	Some creative structures; good variety	Generally interesting sentences; some variety	Choppy sentences; no variety	Fragments, run-on sentences
Conventions	Excellent control and accuracy	Good control with only minor errors	Reasonable control; some errors	Errors that may prevent understanding	Frequent errors that affect meaning

Rubric	4	3	2	1
Focus/Ideas	Clear, focused ad that motivates reader	Clear, interesting ad	Ad with few details and/or lack of focus	Ad lacking clarity and development
Organization/ Paragraphs	Logical, creative, easy to follow	Logical structure	Structure not clear	Lacks organization
Voice	Engaging, provocative	Enthusiasm about subject evident	Weak voice	No enthusiasm or interest evident
Word Choice	Specific, persuasive words; dynamic copy	Good sense of writing to persuade	Some vague, repetitive, or incorrect words	Incorrect, limited word choice
Sentences	Sentence structures varied, creative	Control over simple sentence structures	Choppy sentences; no variety	Fragments, run-on sentences
Conventions	Excellent control and accuracy	Reasonable control with few errors	Errors that may prevent understanding	Frequent errors that affect meaning

Rubric	6	5	4	3	2	1
Focus/Ideas	Topic sentence that clearly explains symbol; strong support	Topic sentence that explains symbol; good details	Topic sentence about symbol; some supporting details	Symbol unclear; needs more supporting details	Symbol undeveloped; few supporting details	Lacks clarity and development of symbol
Organization/ Paragraphs	Well-organized support for topic sentences	Mostly organized support for topic sentences	Topic sentences with some organized support	Support for topic sentences not well organized	Tends to stray; confused or absent topic sentences	Lacks organization, topic sentences
Voice	Engaging, lively, insightful	Generally engaging; good insight	Fairly involved; some insight	Interested but not fully engaged	Tries to show interest in subject	Not involved with subject
Word Choice	Specific, convincing words	Clear, mostly convincing words	Some specific words; generally convincing	Few specific words; not very convincing	Some vague, repetitive, or incorrect words	Incorrect or limited word choice
Sentences	Structures varied, interesting, smooth	Good variety; generally smooth	Correct sentences; some variety	Mostly correct sentences; little variety	Choppy sentences; lacks variety	Fragments, run-on sentences
Conventions	Excellent control and accuracy	Good control with only minor errors	Reasonable control with few serious errors	Some serious errors	Errors that may prevent understanding	Frequent errors that affect meaning

Rubric	5	4	3	2	1
Focus/Ideas	Topic sentence that clearly explains symbol; strong support	Topic sentence that explains symbol; good details	Topic sentence about symbol; some supporting details	Symbol undeveloped; few supporting details	Lacks clarity and development of symbol
Organization/ Paragraphs	Well-organized support for topic sentences	Mostly organized support for topic sentences	Topic sentences with some organized support	Tends to stray; confused or absent topic sentences	Lacks organization, topic sentences
Voice	Engaging, lively, insightful	Generally engaging; good insight	Fairly involved; some insight	Tries to show interest in subject	Not involved with subject
Word Choice	Specific, convincing words	Clear, mostly convincing words	Some specific words; generally convincing	Some vague, repetitive, or incorrect words	Incorrect or limited word choice
Sentences	Structures varied, interesting, smooth	Good variety; generally smooth	Correct sentences; some variety	Choppy sentences; lacks variety	Fragments, run-on sentences
Conventions	Excellent control and accuracy	Good control with only minor errors	Reasonable control with few serious errors	Errors that may prevent understanding	Frequent errors that affect meaning

Rubric	4	3	2	1
Focus/Ideas	Topic sentence that clearly explains symbol; strong support	Topic sentence about symbol; good details	Symbol undeveloped; few supporting details	Lacks clarity and development of symbol
Organization/ Paragraphs	Well-organized support for topic sentences	Topic sentences with organized support	Tends to stray; confused or absent topic sentences	Lacks organization, topic sentences
Voice	Engaging, lively, insightful	Shows interest in subject	Tries to show interest in subject	Not involved with subject
Word Choice	Specific, convincing words	Clear, mostly convincing words	Some vague, repetitive, or incorrect words	Incorrect or limited word choice
Sentences	Structures varied, interesting	Controls simple sentence structures	Choppy sentences; lacks variety	Fragments, run-on sentences
Conventions	Excellent control and accuracy	Reasonable control with few errors	Errors that may prevent understanding	Frequent errors that affect meaning

Rubric	6	5	4	3	2	1
Focus/Ideas	Notes relevant, clear, focused on topic	Notes mostly clear, focused; relevant details included	Notes generally clear; most relevant details included	Notes sometimes off topic; some relevant details	Some irrelevant notes; poor focus on topic	Much irrelevant material; ideas unclear
Organization/ Paragraphs	Notes in written order; rewritten logically	Order of notes mostly logical	Notes in generally logical order	Gaps in notes; affects order	Order of notes not logical	Lacks organization
Voice	Factual; succinct	Factual; generally succinct	Reasonably factual and succinct	Not always objective; sometimes wordy	Wordy; subjective	Too close to source's voice
Word Choice	Concise; uses own words; quotes marked	Mostly concise; uses own words; quotes marked	Mostly uses own words; quotes marked	Little use of own words; quotes not marked	Too many direct quotes	Word-for-word copy
Sentences	Understandable notes; clear fragments	Mostly understandable notes; clear fragments	Generally clear and understandable notes	Sometimes confusing notes and fragments	Unclear fragments	Incomprehensible notes
Conventions	Excellent control and accuracy	Good control; minor errors	Reasonable control with few serious errors	Some serious errors	Errors that may prevent understanding	Frequent errors that affect meaning

Rubric	5	4	3	2	1
Focus/Ideas	Notes relevant, clear, focused on topic	Notes mostly clear, focused; relevant details included	Notes generally clear; most relevant details included	Some irrelevant notes; poor focus on topic	Much irrelevant material; ideas unclear
Organization/ Paragraphs	Notes in written order; rewritten logically	Order of notes mostly logical	Notes in generally logical order	Order of notes not logical	Lacks organization
Voice	Factual; succinct	Factual; generally succinct	Reasonably factual and succinct	Wordy; subjective	Too close to source's voice
Word Choice	Concise; uses own words; quotes marked	Mostly concise; uses own words; quotes marked	Mostly uses own words; quotes marked	Too many direct quotes; not marked	Word-for-word copy
Sentences	Understandable notes; clear fragments	Mostly understandable notes; clear fragments	Generally clear and understandable notes	Unclear fragments	Incomprehensible notes
Conventions	Excellent control and accuracy	Good control; minor errors	Reasonable control with few serious errors	Errors that may prevent understanding	Frequent errors that affect meaning

Rubric	4	3	2	1
Focus/Ideas	Notes relevant, clear, focused on topic	Notes reasonably focused; relevant details included	Some irrelevant notes; poor focus on topic	Much irrelevant material; ideas unclear
Organization/ Paragraphs	Notes in written order; rewritten logically	Order of notes mostly logical	Order of notes not logical	Lacks organization
Voice	Factual; succinct	Factual; generally succinct	Wordy; subjective	Too close to source's voice
Word Choice	Concise; uses own words; quotes marked	Specific choices; closer to source	Too many direct quotes	Word-for-word copy
Sentences	Understandable notes; clear fragments	Clear fragments	Unclear fragments	Incomprehensible notes
Conventions	Excellent control and accuracy	Reasonable control with few errors	Errors that may prevent understanding	Frequent errors that affect meaning

Rubric	6	5	4	3	2	1
Focus/Ideas	Clear, focused newsletter with strong conclusion	Focused newsletter with good conclusion	Mostly focused newsletter; reasonable conclusion	Newsletter focused at times; poor conclusion	Newsletter with weak focus; needs conclusion	Newsletter with no focus or conclusion
Organization/ Paragraphs	Logical order; main ideas followed by details	Order of details logical	Order of details adequate	Some details out of order	Confused order	Lacks order
Voice	Engaging, lively, authoritative	Enthusiastic; involved with subject	Generally engaged and informed	Sincere but uncertain of subject	Tries to be involved with subject	Not involved with subject
Word Choice	Specific words; communicates clearly	Clear words; uses words to set tone	Mostly clear words; tells about subject	Correct words but needs more specific ones	Some vague, repetitive, or incorrect words	Incorrect or limited word choice
Sentences	Structures varied, interesting, smooth	Good variety; generally smooth	Correct sentences; some variety	Mostly correct sentences; little variety	Choppy sentences; lacks variety	Fragments, run-on sentences
Conventions	Excellent control and accuracy	Good control with only minor errors	Reasonable control with few serious errors	Some serious errors	Errors that may prevent understanding	Frequent errors that affect meaning

Rubric	5	4	3	2	1
Focus/Ideas	Clear, focused newsletter with strong conclusion	Focused newsletter with good conclusion	Mostly focused newsletter; reasonable conclusion	Newsletter with weak focus and conclusion	Newsletter with no focus or conclusion
Organization/ Paragraphs	Logical order; main ideas followed by details	Order of details logical	Order of details adequate	Confused order	Lacks order
Voice	Engaging, lively, authoritative	Enthusiastic; involved with subject	Generally engaged and informed	Tries to be involved with subject	Not involved with subject
Word Choice	Specific words; communicates clearly	Clear words; uses words to set tone	Mostly clear words; tells about subject	Some vague, repetitive, or incorrect words	Incorrect or limited word choice
Sentences	Structures varied, interesting, smooth	Good variety; generally smooth	Correct sentences; some variety	Choppy sentences; lacks variety	Fragments, run-on sentences
Conventions	Excellent control and accuracy	Good control with only minor errors	Reasonable control with few serious errors	Errors that may prevent understanding	Frequent errors that affect meaning

Rubric	4	3	2	1
Focus/Ideas	Clear, focused newsletter with strong conclusion	Reasonably well-focused newsletter with good conclusion	Newsletter with weak focus and conclusion	Newsletter with no focus or conclusion
Organization/ Paragraphs	Logical order; main ideas followed by details	Order mostly logical	Confused order	Lacks order
Voice	Engaging, lively, authoritative	Writer involved with subject	Tries to be involved with subject	Not involved with subject
Word Choice	Specific words; communicates clearly	Clear; uses words to set tone	Some vague, repetitive, or incorrect words	Incorrect or limited word choice
Sentences	Structures varied, interesting	Control over simple sentence structures	Choppy sentences; lacks variety	Fragments, run-on sentences
Conventions	Excellent control and accuracy	Reasonable control with few errors	Errors that may prevent understanding	Frequent errors that affect meaning

Rubric	6	5	4	3	2	1
Focus/Ideas	Clear, focused, comprehensive outline	Focused, inclusive outline	Outline with most important information included	Outline with some important information missing	Outline with much important information missing	Outline with most information missing
Organization/ Paragraphs	Excellent control of outline format; items in proper order	Correct outline format; items in order of reading	Correct outline format; items in mostly proper order	Uneven use of outline format; some items out of order	Tends to stray from outline format; items out of order	Outline format confused and disorganized
Voice	Writer fully engaged; uses own voice	Writer involved with subject; uses own voice	Generally engaged; mostly uses own voice	Somewhat involved; often does not use own voice	Tries to be involved but derivative	Not involved
Word Choice	Specific; gives precision to facts	Mostly specific and clear	Some specific words	Many direct quotations; general words	Too many direct quotations	Closely copied from original text
Sentences	Clear sentences or heads	Mostly clear sentences or heads	Generally clear sentences or heads	Some clear sentences or heads	Few clear sentences or heads	Many unclear sentences and heads
Conventions	Excellent control and accuracy	Good control with only minor errors	Reasonable control with few serious errors	Some serious errors	Errors that may prevent understanding	Frequent errors that affect meaning

Rubric	5	4	3	2	1
Focus/Ideas	Clear, focused, comprehensive outline	Focused, inclusive outline	Generally focused outline with most ideas	Outline with some information missing	Outline with most information missing
Organization/ Paragraphs	Excellent control of outline format; items in proper order	Correct outline format; items in order of reading	Correct outline format; items in mostly proper order	Tends to stray from outline format; items out of order	Outline format confused; information chaotic
Voice	Writer fully engaged; uses own voice	Writer involved with subject; uses own voice	Generally engaged; mostly uses own voice	Tries to be involved with subject; derivative	Not involved; no sense of person
Word Choice	Specific; gives precision to facts	Mostly specific and clear	Some specific words	Too many direct quotations	Closely copied from original text
Sentences	Clear sentences or heads	Mostly clear sentences or heads	Generally clear sentences or heads	Some sentences and heads unclear	Many unclear sentences and heads
Conventions	Excellent control and accuracy	Good control with only minor errors	Reasonable control with few serious errors	Errors that may prevent understanding	Frequent errors that affect meaning

Rubric	4	3	2	1
Focus/Ideas	Clear, focused, comprehensive outline	Reasonably focused, inclusive outline	Outline with some information missing	Outline with most information missing
Organization/ Paragraphs	Excellent control of outline format; proper order	Mostly uses correct outline format; proper order	Tends to stray from outline format	Outline format confused and disorganized
Voice	Writer fully engaged; uses own voice	Writer involved with subject	Tries to be involved with subject; derivative	Not involved
Word Choice	Specific; gives precision to facts	Mostly specific and clear	Too many direct quotations	Closely copied from original text
Sentences	Clear sentences or heads	Mostly clear sentences or heads	Some sentences and heads unclear	Many unclear sentences and heads
Conventions	Excellent control and accuracy	Reasonable control with few errors	Errors that may prevent understanding	Frequent errors that affect meaning

Rubric	6	5	4	3	2	1
Focus/Ideas	Clear, focused job application essay	Focused job application essay	Generally focused job application essay	Job application essay with reasonable focus	Job application essay that strays from topic	Job application essay lacking clarity and focus
Organization/Paragraphs	Uses logical order; main ideas, then relevant details	Mostly uses logical order; main ideas, then useful details	Acceptable order; main ideas, then details	Main ideas, then mix of useful and irrelevant details	Somewhat disorganized; irrelevant details	Lacks organization and appropriate information
Voice	Engaging, lively; shows individuality	Writer involved with subject; personality evident	Shows some involvement and personality	Somewhat involved but no individuality	Tries to be involved with subject	Not involved with subject
Word Choice	Specific words that reveal qualifications	Mostly clear words that describe character traits	Some specific words that tell about qualifications	Few specific words; no clear picture of applicant	Some vague, repetitive, or incorrect words	Incorrect or limited word choice
Sentences	Structures varied; create clarity and interest	Structures good; mostly varied, interesting	Correct sentences; some variety	Correct but mostly simple sentences; little variety	Choppy sentences; lacks variety	Fragments, run-on sentences
Conventions	Excellent control and accuracy	Good control with only minor errors	Reasonable control with few serious errors	Some serious errors	Errors that may prevent understanding	Frequent errors that affect meaning

Rubric	5	4	3	2	1
Focus/Ideas	Clear, focused job application essay	Reasonably well-focused job application essay	Generally focused job application essay	Job application essay that strays from topic	Job application essay lacking clarity and focus
Organization/Paragraphs	Uses logical order; main ideas, then relevant details	Mostly uses logical order; main ideas, then useful details	Acceptable order; main ideas, then details	Somewhat disorganized; irrelevant details	Lacks organization and appropriate information
Voice	Engaging, lively; shows individuality	Writer involved with subject; personality evident	Shows some involvement and personality	Tries to be involved with subject	Not involved with subject
Word Choice	Specific words that reveal qualifications	Mostly clear words that describe character traits	Some specific words that tell about qualifications	Some vague, repetitive, or incorrect words	Incorrect or limited word choice
Sentences	Structures varied; create clarity and interest	Structures good; mostly varied, interesting	Correct sentences; some variety	Choppy sentences; lacks variety	Fragments, run-on sentences
Conventions	Excellent control and accuracy	Good control with only minor errors	Reasonable control with few serious errors	Errors that may prevent understanding	Frequent errors that affect meaning

Rubric	4	3	2	1
Focus/Ideas	Clear, focused job application essay	Reasonably well-focused job application essay	Job application essay that strays from topic	Job application essay lacking clarity and focus
Organization/Paragraphs	Uses logical order; main ideas, then relevant details	Mostly uses logical order; useful details	Somewhat disorganized; irrelevant details	Lacks organization and appropriate information
Voice	Engaging, lively; shows individuality	Writer involved with subject; personality evident	Tries to be involved with subject	Not involved with subject
Word Choice	Specific words that reveal qualifications	Some specific words that reveal qualifications	Some vague, repetitive, or incorrect words	Incorrect or limited word choice
Sentences	Structures varied; interesting	Control over simple sentence structures	Choppy sentences; lacks variety	Fragments, run-on sentences
Conventions	Excellent control and accuracy	Reasonable control with few errors	Errors that may prevent understanding	Frequent errors that affect meaning

Writing Models

PROMPT Think of a friend, relative, or pet you care about and feel loyalty toward. Write a personal narrative about an incident that shows you cared or were cared for. Describe the situation, who was involved, and how you felt as a result.

Birthday Ice Cream

Last March Mrs. Vilanese said that she had gotten too old and that Rascal had gotten too rambunctious to keep. That's how I got my dog. Did you know that dogs have personalities? Rascal sure does! He always wags his stumpy tail and howls at ambulance sirens. You might not believe this, but he even smiles.

Mrs. Vilanese was right though. He is rambunctious. Last May was my eleventh birthday. Our family has this tradition. Whoever has the birthday gets to choose the cake and the meal for dinner. Mom made me a carrot cake with orange frosting—my favorite. She put it on the kitchen counter to cool.

While the cake was cooling, I shot baskets at Lemoyne School with Ricky, Jason, and Brett. Then we all came to my house for dinner. When we barged in the door, the first thing I saw was the cake plate on the floor. No cake! No crumbs! Rascal was wagging his stump and looking fat. He smelled like orange frosting. I yelled, "Oh, no, you didn't eat my cake, Rascal!" He did not smile.

Continued on next page

> After the cake disaster, we finally ate pizza and salad. Afterwards, we had ice cream balls with candles stuck in them. It was a pretty crazy birthday, but I still love Rascal. Now we have another birthday tradition. We serve ice cream balls with candles. And Mom always puts the cake on top of the fridge to cool.

Score 4

Narrative is well focused on Rascal and his effect on the narrator's birthday. The writer makes smooth transitions at the beginning of paragraphs two, three, and four and uses time-order words. Humor, vivid details, and a quotation give readers a sense of "being there." Lively words *(rambunctious, stumpy, sirens, barged)* appeal to readers' emotions or senses. Compound and complex sentences contribute to fluency. There is good control of conventions.

Think of a friend, relative, or pet you care about and feel loyalty toward. Write a personal narrative about an incident that shows you cared or were cared for. Describe the situation, who was involved, and how you felt as a result.

Me, My Dad, and My Broken Leg

I broke my leg when I was nine years old. I was swinging on my tire swing. When suddenly the rope came lose. I soared through the clear, blue sky. I hit the cold, hard ground. My dad heard my piercing cries and rushed me to the hospital. In the car he told jokes. "Wait until I get home," he said. "That swing is grounded for a month!" I couldn't help but laugh.

When we arrived at the hospital, Dad carefully scooped up my trembling body and carried me inside. As we waited for the doctor, I squeezed Dad's hand. He squeezed back gently and winked. Then the doctor came in and explained that she had to straighten my twisted leg before she could set it in a cast. My stomach dropped. Suddenly, Dad yelled, "Wow!" I whipped my head around to see what was happening. Dad said, "Done!" and smiled. I looked back at my leg. It was straight, and the doctor was already preparing the cast!

Finally, it was time to go home. I didn't know how to use my new crutches. I was afraid of looking foolish. So you know what Dad did? He asked the nurse if he could

Continued on next page

> have some crutches too! Together we fumbled and zig-
> zagged our way to the car.
>   My dad has always supported me, but on that day he
> was there when I needed him most. His humor and care
> helped me through a painful and scary experience. If my
> dad ever needs me, I know I'll be there for him too.

Score 3

This narrative captures a special event and expresses the writer's feelings
about it. Voice is earnest and appealing. Word choice is precise. Sentences
are generally fluent. Some short sentences beginning with *I* in paragraphs
one and three could be combined for smoother reading. There is a fragment
and a misspelled word in paragraph one, sentence three.

PROMPT Think of a friend, relative, or pet you care about and feel loyalty toward. Write a personal narrative about an incident that shows you cared or were cared for. Describe the situation, who was involved, and how you felt as a result.

No Hands

Never try to ride a bike without any hands. My mom always told me to be careful on my bike, but did I listen to her, no. Whenever I went out she always told me to ride with both hands, wear a helmet, and look both ways before crossing the street. I never got hurt until the accident.

It was November 4th, my birthday. My parents got me a really nice bike. It was pink with yellow and it felt smoth and looked shiney and sparkly. I loved it! I loved it so much I rode almost every day. I was pretty good at it, I could do tricks and ride really fast. That's until the accident.

It was a nice fall evening, and the breeze was really relaxing. There were so many trees at the park that it made a lot of wind. So when I rode my bike I felt all the wind in my face as if I had a enormous fan blown on me. When I looked back to see if my parents were there, I saw a guy riding his bike without any hands, it looked easy, so I tried it. I started to peddle, then I lifted one hand off the handle and then the other. I started to ride my bike without any hands, and suddenly I lost

Continued on next page

balance and Ka-Boom! I hit the side of the tree and scraped my elbows and knees.

Seconds later my mom was helping me get up. My father put the bike in the car and drove us home. My mother got the first-aid kit. She started cleaning my knees. My knees looked like they just caught on fire, it burned really bad. They were also bleeding a lot. When my mom was finished I thanked her so much. I told her, "Mom, I will never, ever, ever ride a bike without any hands, I promise." The next morning I woked to see that my knees were a little bit better. I'm so glad I have a mother who cares about me.

I still ride my bike, but now I listen to my mom a little bit more. I don't think I'll ever ride a bike without any hands ever again. I will always be loyal to my mom. I will always remember that day.

Score 2

This narrative addresses the prompt and conveys the writer's personality. The opening command immediately engages readers. Some strong words *(enormous fan blown on me, Ka-Boom, scraped, like they just caught on fire)* and a quote enliven the writing. The word *really* is overused. Run-on sentences, usage errors *(a enormous, I woked)*, and misspellings *(smoth, shiney, peddle)* detract from the piece.

PROMPT Think of a friend, relative, or pet you care about and feel loyalty toward. Write a personal narrative about an incident that shows you cared or were cared for. Describe the situation, who was involved, and how you felt as a result.

Let's Talk

My best friend and I have known each other for five years. We weren't friends at first though. We didn't even like each other for the first year and a half. But then we both started to accept each other. We learned how to put up with each other's attitudes and differing opinions. Since then we have been inseparable.

Together my friend and I learned a lesson on saying what we think to each other even if we might differ in opinion. We know that even if we disagree we will still be friends. It started in the 4th grade when I was sick. While I was sick my best friend became friends with another girl. When I came back all my friend did was talk about her so I also became friends with the girl. We kept on hanging out with her so we all became really good friends.

For the rest of the year we were known as "The Three Musketeers" because we were so close. So at the end of the year we were all hoping for the same teacher at our new school. But although my best friend and I were together we weren't with the other girl. I wasn't to disappointed because I was on the same bus as her and I wanted to be with my other friend more than being with her.

Continued on next page

For a while the girl and I were always on the bus talking to each other. But then the girl got new friends. After telling my best friend about how the girl didn't really talk to me anymore my best friend admitted that she didn't really like the girl and only hanged out with her because she thought that I really wanted to be friends with her. I was so surprised that my friend cared so much about me she spent a year hanging out with someone she didn't really like! I told my friend that I only hanged out with the girl because I thought that she really wanted to be friends with her. And we both started to laugh.

Now we never do talk to that girl anymore. Instead we became best friends with another girl who we both liked. We still are friends with her and even closer to our new friend then with our old one. My friend and I now both express our feelings with each other because even disagreeing is better then assuming what each other thinks.

Score 1

This narrative would be more effective if it were less wordy and used more precise words. The situation is too general and lacks specific details such as names, places, and description. Words are vague and repetitive. Conventions errors include an incorrect verb form *(hanged out)*, misspellings *(to* for *too, then* for *than)*, incorrect pronouns *(I was on the same bus as her; who we both liked)*, and missing commas in compound and complex sentences.

Write a report that gives steps on how to make or do something. Make your report interesting to read and easy to understand. Explain all the steps and materials needed.

How to Make a Constellation Map

Materials: pictures of constellations, tracing paper, cardboard, pen, marker, ruler, flashlight

You can map the stars in a constellation. This map will help you find the constellation among the stars in the dark night sky.

First, select one picture of a constellation. Cover the picture with tracing paper and trace the lines that connect the stars.

Next, place the tracing paper over the cardboard and punch holes in it with a pen where the stars appear (where the lines connect). Use the ruler to draw straight lines connecting the holes. Then label the cardboard with the name of the constellation. You may want to write notes on the cardboard, such as how the constellation got its name.

Finally, take the cardboard and a flashlight into a dark place, such as a closet. Hold the constellation map with the side you worked on facing down. Hold the flashlight under the map and shine the light up. You will see the constellation reflected on the ceiling.

Continued on next page

Score 4

Report focuses on one activity and explains it clearly. Writer lists materials and provides an introduction. Steps are explained clearly and succinctly, using time-order words such as *first, next, then,* and *finally*. Strong verbs *(select, trace, punch, label)* tell what to do. Sentences are fluent and concise, with varying lengths. The report shows a good understanding of writing conventions.

PROMPT

Write a report that gives steps on how to make or do something. Make your report interesting to read and easy to understand. Explain all the steps and materials needed.

How to Make a Mobius Strip

Materiels: 8 1/2" x 14" sheet of paper, scissors, tape, pen

Do you know how to make a strip of paper that has only one side? Listen carefully and I'll tell you how to construct a Mobius strip. Then you can impress your friends with this clever construction.

First, cut a strip of paper one inch wide from the long side of your paper. Then make the two ends of the strip meet in a circle. Next, turn one end over. Tape the overlapping ends together. The first time I tried to make a Mobius strip, I forgot to turn one end over, and I found out that it spoiled the whole thing.

Here's how you prove that your Mobius strip has only one side. Place a side of the strip on a flat table. Then with your pen mark a continuious line on the strip. Don't take your pen off the paper. Extend the line until you come to the place where you started.

Ask your friends to explain your one-sided paper. Can they figure it out.

Continued on next page

Score 3

This report provides clear steps and uses precise words. The initial question engages readers, and the explanation of how to prove that the strip has only one side adds interest to the report. The last sentence in paragraph two strays from the actual steps. Two spelling errors *(Materiels, continuious)* and incorrect punctuation of the final sentence in the report do not seriously detract from the piece.

PROMPT

Write a report that gives steps on how to make or do something. Make your report interesting to read and easy to understand. Explain all the steps and materials needed.

How to Make a Hemp Bracelet

If you want to make a hemp bracelet, first you have to get some hemp. Different bracelet styles require different amounts of hemp. For instance Spiral Hemp Bracelets require two pieces of 7 1/2 feet of hemp. A Ripple Hemp bracelet would need two pieces of 5 feet of hemp. It also depends on how big in size the person's wrist is. Every time you cut a piece of hemp you should probably add a little more to make sure it fits. Some bracelets can also have beads added on.

One of the easiest bracelets to make is the spiral. To make it you need two pieces of hemp each 7 1/2 feet in length. Then take both pieces and fold them in half. After that make a loop knot at the half mark. This should leave four pieces of hemp of equal length hanging down. Take the two middle pieces and lay them next to each other. Put the other two pieces to the side. Then take the piece farthest to the left and cross it over the two middle strands and under the strand on the right.

Now take the right strand and put it under the two middle strands and over the left one. Next pull both

Continued on next page

outside strands to start the design. Repeat the step to create a repeating spiral pattern. Make it as long as wanted. To end the pattern take all four strands of hemp and tie them into a knot. The knot should fit into the loop made on the other end. Put it onto your wrist and your done.

If you think you're bracelet looks to plain then here is a way to add more style to it. Start the bracelet by creating the loop knot. Make the bracelet as long as wanted and then pull one of the middle strands up. Continue the pattern and then put some beads on the strand you pulled up. Pull the strand back down and continue the pattern. You should now have some beads in the middle of the bracelet. You can repeat this and have as many beads as you want on your hemp bracelet.

The spiral hemp bracelet is a great bracelet to start out with if your new to bracelet making. It's simple and looks great. It's also easy if you want to experiment with it. If wanted more hemp can be added to make anklets or necklaces. Now that you know how to make the spiral hemp bracelet continue on to other designs!

Continued on next page

Score 2

Wordiness seriously detracts from this how-to report. (For example, *big in size* instead of *big, feet in length* instead *of feet)* Steps are not always precise. Errors include confusing homonyms *(your* and *you're, to* and *too)*, incorrect capitalization, and missing commas.

Write a report that gives steps on how to make or do something. Make your report interesting to read and easy to understand. Explain all the steps and materials needed.

Blowing Bubbles

Its easy to blow a bubble. First you must have bubblegum and a mouth. Chew the gum for a little wile. Now push your tung against it and stick it out of you're mouth. HURRY UP and blow before it closes up but dont blow to hard or it will fly out of your mouth and you get stuff sticked all over your face! That happened to my little brother all the time.

Score 1

Pervasive errors determine this low score. Errors include many misspellings, an over-connected sentence *(HURRY…face!)*, lack of paragraph indention, and incorrect verb forms.

PROMPT Compare and contrast two successful people you have read or heard about. Choose real people or fictional characters who have achieved great things or solved problems. Tell about important similarities or differences.

A Breakthrough in Science

Many women have struggled to get into the field of science and then to receive recognition for their efforts. Two famous pioneers in science, Marie Curie and Elizabeth Blackwell, faced different barriers along their roads to success. In the end, both women made an impact on future female scientists.

Marie Curie's main obstacle was financial. As a teenager, Curie worked as a teacher and governess to support her family. Later, after hard work and study, she attended the Sorbonne, a selective school in Paris. For Curie's work in chemistry and physics, she received two Nobel prizes. Through her dedication, she showed that women scientists could achieve greatness.

Elizabeth Blackwell faced a different obstacle: discrimination. Unlike Curie, Blackwell had trouble getting into school. American medical schools did not accept women. However, Blackwell persisted and was finally admitted to medical school. She eventually received her medical degree, founded an infirmary, and wrote important scientific articles. Like Curie, Blackwell inspired women to follow in her footsteps.

Continued on next page

> Both Marie Curie and Elizabeth Blackwell had to overcome obstacles to achieve their goals in science. They devoted their lives to the cause and influenced generations to come.

Score 4

Essay is focused and well elaborated. There is a logical structure: The introduction identifies the two subjects being compared; the body compares the subjects; the conclusion summarizes the comparisons. Writer maintains a respectful tone toward the subjects. Specific words (*governess, chemistry, physics, infirmary*) and precise transitions (*both, unlike, however, like*) are used. Varied sentence structures make the writing pleasant to read. There is a good control of conventions.

PROMPT

Compare and contrast two successful people you have read or heard about. Choose real people or fictional characters who have achieved great things or solved problems. Tell about important similarities or differences.

Overcoming Obstacles

Talented young people often set out to achieve a goal, but they sometimes have a hard time achieving that goal because of the fact that there are obstacles. Elizabeth Blackwell and Marian Anderson were both women who rose above obstacles that got in their way. They realized their dreams through patience and dedication.

Elizabeth Blackwell's gender was the major obstacle to attaining her dream. Colleges and hospitals rejected her because she was a woman. This prejudice because of her gender could have prevented her from pursuing her goal. Yet Blackwell overcame this obstacle. Instead of giving up, she continued to follow her passion. Eventually, she became a famous doctor and also a pioneer in the medical profession.

Another woman who overcame prejudice was Marian Anderson. Anderson had a beautiful singing voice. She performed all over the world, except in her home country, which was the United States. People knew she had a great amount of talent, but the problem was that she was black. Marian persevered and sang in other countries despite this obstacle. Finally, Marian was invited to sing

Continued on next page

on the steps of the Lincoln Memorial. She became the first African American to sing in a public place that was previously labeled "for white performers only."

These two women overcame different obstacles in different ways. Yet they both sent an important message about persistance and the need for equal treatment of all people.

Score 3

This compare and contrast essay explains the obstacles these two women faced and the qualities that enabled them to attain their goals. However, wordiness (for example, the initial sentence, along with phrases such as *obstacles that got in their way*) detracts from the writing. There is a reasonable control over conventions except for a spelling error *(persistance)*.

PROMPT Compare and contrast two successful people you have read or heard about. Choose real people or fictional characters who have achieved great things or solved problems. Tell about important similarities or differences.

Thomas Edison and Alexander Bell

Thomas Edison and Alexander Bell created two of the greatest inventions ever invented within three years of each other. Edison invented the light bulb in 1879 and Bell invented the telephone in 1876. Both inventions are still commonly used today.

Both inventors had rivals. A scientist in England, Joseph Wilson Swan, was also trying to invent the light bulb at the same time as Thomas Edison. Elisha Gray and Alexander Bell both were racing to invent the telephone in the U.S. Joseph Swan actually did make the first light bulb but had troubles on keeping the light going at all times. Edison fixed those problems and patented his design. Elisha Gray and Bell patented their telephone designs on the same day but Bell's design arrived to the New York patent office two hours before Elisha Gray's did but it doesn't say why the delay.

Edison and Bell were both born into middle class families and had siblings. They also both caught serious dieses. Bell caught tuberculosis, which his two brothers died from, but Alexander recovered from. Edison had dieses with a high fever that caused him some loss of hearing. However they lived very far apart. Edison was

Continued on next page

born and raised in America. Bell was born in Scotland and than moved to Canada in his childhood. Later in Bell's life he would move to America. Another similarity between the two inventers is that even at a young age they both loved to read and experiment with things that helped them later become inventors.

Even while inventing Bell and Edison had assistants. Bell had an assistant named Watson. Edison had a whole group of men helping him. But they did experiments in different ways. At the time of making the light bulb Edison had a day-job at a telegraph office. He did most of his experimenting at night, not in the day. Bell however spent all of his time creating the telephone. Both men were also married and had kids.

Edison and Bell were two different men that shared similar interests and some similar background. Our lives would be very different without these two men inventing things we use all the time.

Score 2

This essay addresses the prompt and uses words such as *both* and *also* to compare. Many sentences are wordy or awkward, which noticeably detracts from the work. Some facts stray from the topic or are repeated. In addition, lack of punctuation and several misspellings help account for the score.

PROMPT

Compare and contrast two successful people you have read or heard about. Choose real people or fictional characters who have achieved great things or solved problems. Tell about important similarities or differences.

Two Astromoners

Giovanni Battista Donati and Galileo were one of the many people I learned about while studing astronomy. I love to read about astronomy and how the universe formed. So while I was reading I found Donati and Galileo and I thought they were interesting. Giovanni Battista Donati was born at Pisa, Italy. He was a astronomer and became a proffesor at the Royal Institute and then the directer of an observatory in Florance. He discovered six comets, and one is named after him. Galileo was born near Pisa, Italy on February 15, 1564. He was a Italian physicist and a astronomer. He discovered about falling bodies & gravity. Some other things he learned were about sunspots, luner mountains, valleys, the four largest moons of Jupiter, the phases of venus. He discovered all of that with a telescope that he builded. He builded a telescope with a magnification of twenty lenses. Both Donati and Galileo were Italians and they also discovered something that has helped us all. There are probly other comparisons that I don't even know about. These two men are very interesting and I am glad I read about them for a research report.

Continued on next page

Score 1

This report tells a few things about these two men rather than focusing on comparing and contrasting them. The one sentences that attempts to make a comparison *(Both Donati and Galileo…helped us all.)* is too general to be effective. Writing is wordy and repetitive. Many sentences begin with *He.* There are many mechanical errors, including misspellings, usage errors *(builded* for *built, a* rather than *an* before words beginning with vowels), and lack of punctuation and paragraphing.

Write a story about an adventure, a discovery, or something that happened for the first time. Use some of these literary devices: foreshadowing, tension, suspense, conflict, humor.

Trip to Planet X

Suddenly the satellite's signal disappeared from the screen. We had followed satellite GX17 since it was knocked out of its orbit by a meteoroid. The satellite carried valuable instruments and data, and we needed to find it. It couldn't have just disappeared. Jackson and I had to find out what really happened to GX17.

We flew toward where we had last seen the satellite's signal. After many hours, an orange mass came into view. It appeared to be a very small planet. Had the satellite hit the planet? We didn't know. But exploring this mysterious place was an opportunity Jackson and I couldn't pass up.

We were trembling with anticipation as we stepped out onto the planet. All around us were deep orange craters and wide valleys. The sky was a pale yellow without a single cloud. We spotted part of the satellite 100 yards away and hiked toward it.

The satellite was in pieces. Luckily, the recording equipment was unharmed. We took photos of the planet with the satellite's camera and collected a soil sample. We needed proof to take home. Our suits were running low on oxygen; it was time to head back to the ship.

Continued on next page

> On the way home, Jackson and I could not keep the smiles off our faces. Not only did we find the satellite, but we had discovered something extraordinary—an unknown planet.

Score 4

Story is focused on the quest to find the lost satellite. Paragraphs are smoothly connected. Writer uses literary elements such as foreshadowing, suspense, and conflict to make the story exciting. Specific words and vivid imagery keep the reader interested. Varied sentence lengths and structures create a rhythm that fits the action in the story. Writer has excellent control of grammar, capitalization, spelling, and punctuation.

Write a story about an adventure, a discovery, or something that happened for the first time. Use some of these literary devices: foreshadowing, tension, suspense, conflict, humor.

The Mystery in the Barn

As my sister Abby and I approached the barn, chills ran up my spine. Its just the old weathered barn behind Grandma's house, I thought. But I feared what might be in it. Grandma always kept the barn doors tightly locked. What could be inside?

Grandma was making dinner, but she would be wondering where we were. We didn't want to worry her, so we had to hurry. I yanked a loose board on the side of the barn, and Abby wiggled inside. At first, Abby was silent. Then she yelled Whoa! I helped her squeeze back through the boards.

"What did you see" I asked excitedly?

"You know that car you and Dad are always talking about? The red convertible? Well, its in there under a dusty tarp." I couldnt believe it! Grandma had been keeping a sports car in her barn?

Just then we heard footsteps. Abby and I tried to run and hide, but Grandma had seen us. "Isn't it a great gift" she said? A gift for who? I wondered. It turned out that the car had been Grandpa's. It had got all grungy since he died. Grandma had it restored as a birthday

Continued on next page

surprise for our dad. Abby and me would keep her

secret. I couldn't wait for Dad to discover the mystery

inside the barn for himself.

Score 3

This story is lively and well paced. The first paragraph develops a mood
of suspense to build up to the discovery of the car. Word choice is precise
(weathered, yanked, wiggled). A few errors prevent the story from receiving
a top score. Some contractions are misspelled, quotations are sometimes
incorrectly punctuated, and there are two pronoun errors. *(A gift for <u>who</u>?
Abby and <u>me</u> would keep her secret.)*

Write a story about an adventure, a discovery, or something that happened for the first time. Use some of these literary devices: foreshadowing, tension, suspense, conflict, humor.

Mount Lemon

One of the scariest moments of my life was when I got lost on Mount Lemon with my dad. He said we were only going to hike for just a couple of hours. When we were hiking up, it started to get dark, and we were running out of water. I told my dad we should find some water.

It was already dark, so we couldn't see much and the only source of light we had was the moon and that wasn't very bright either. We finally found a place to drink water and rest. I asked Dad if we were lost and unfortunately he said yes. I checked to see what time it was and it was 8:00 o clock. I asked Dad if we should call my mom and tell her what happened. The bad part was, we only had ten minutes left on our cell phone, so we made it quick.

My mom called the rescue people to come rescue us. Thank goodness! I thought we would live on the mountain forever. Dad and I had to climb all the way to the top of the mountain for the people to rescue us. We finally reached the top. I was so tierd, I could barely move. I was leaning against a rock, shivering from the coldness and dieing of hungryness. Then I suddenly felt

Continued on next page

something. It was slimy and kind of rough at the same time. I turned to look back and there it was, a bronze colored rattlesnake! I must have jumped 10 feet in the air. Dad told me not to move, couple minutes later the snake left.

I suddenly felt like I was in Hevan. I looked up to a light moving across the sky. The helicopter had arrived! Dad and I waved to it and then it lowered a rope, I grabed on to it and then we were lifted in the air. When we got home my mom was so worried. She said it must have been really terrible there, it was terrible, but hey at least we got a free helicopter ride!

Score 2

This is a compelling story with some vivid details. The writer creates a mood of tension and suspense, especially in the incident with the rattlesnake. Frequent misspellings, run-on sentences, and capitalization and punctuation errors noticeably detract from the narration. Some sentences are over-connected with *and.* Many sentences begin with *I.*

PROMPT Write a story about an adventure, a discovery, or something that happened for the first time. Use some of these literary devices: foreshadowing, tension, suspense, conflict, humor.

Big Roller

Last year I rode a roller coaster for the first time. It was COOL! We went really fast and really high, and the people on the ground looked small. You feel like you're a king up there. My sister rocked the cage, and that made me really nervous. But it was an awesome experience and is one that I hope to do again.

Score 1

This piece lacks the beginning-middle-end structure and development of a story. The word *really* is overused. Although the piece is free of mechanical errors, it is too sketchy to merit a higher score.

PROMPT

Write a persuasive essay for your classmates about something you would like to change at school. State your suggestion, supporting it with examples and details to convince your readers of your point of view.

Not Enough Time

Our school should add a free period to the schedule. First, students need time with their friends. Second, students require time to get help from teachers. Last, students should have the chance to exercise.

Students need time during the day to see their friends. If you don't have the same classes, you hardly see one another all day. At lunch, everyone is so busy waiting in the line or eating that there's not enough time to even talk. An extra period could allow us to get together. Building friendships is important.

Students often require extra help with homework, and teachers are the best people to give that help. Students could use the free period to get their questions answered. Even better, teachers could set up study sessions during the period to address several students' needs at once.

The most important reason for a free period is to give students a chance to exercise. Exercise would improve overall health. Best of all, we would be more alert during our classes and ready to learn.

Continued on next page

> Students need extra time during the day. With a free period, we could build friendships, get help from teachers, or get some good exercise. Just a few extra minutes would really make a difference!

Score 4

Argument is focused on the topic of adding a free period to the schedule. There is a logical organization, with the writer's opinion stated at the beginning followed by three reasons with supporting details. The most important reason comes last. Writing is formal, appropriate to the form, and sincere. Writer clearly believes in the topic. Persuasive words such as *should, need, even better, most important,* and *best of all* strengthen the argument. The word *get,* which appears often, could be replaced with some stronger verbs. Varied sentence lengths, kinds, and structures create clear and effective communication.

> **PROMPT** **Write a persuasive essay for your classmates about something you would like to change at school. State your suggestion, supporting it with examples and details to convince your readers of your point of view.**

Food for Thought

Our school needs to collect food. Not waste it. First, throwing away uneaten food is wrong. Second, unpeeled fruit, sealed snack packs, and unopened juice and milk containers could be given to students who forget their lunches. Last and most important, the food could be donated to the community.

Many of us have too much or unwanted food for lunch and end up dumping some of it into the garbage. By doing that, we waste valuable resources and money.

The extra food could be used by students at our school. How often have you forgot your lunch? If we collected uneaten food, you could get a replacement lunch. Best of all, you wouldn't have to go hungry. Or borrow money from your friends.

Collected food could also be given to people in the community. What a wonderful way to demonstrate that we care! Each day the food could be put into boxes, and a supervised group of students could deliver them to a shelter. The people who most need the resources will get them, and students get an opportunity to help others.

Continued on next page

> Wasting food hurts everyone, while collecting food for anyone who need it can make a difference. Next time you don't want that apple, please think twice about throwing it away.

Score 3

This persuasive essay makes a convincing case for collecting uneaten lunchroom food. The argument builds logically, and the conclusion provides a strong wrap-up. Voice is committed, and word choice is effective. Different types of sentences add interest and fluency. Two sentence fragments and two incorrect verb forms (*forgot* instead of *forgotten; anyone who _need_ it*) prevent this essay from getting a top score.

PROMPT

Write a persuasive essay for your classmates about something you would like to change at school. State your suggestion, supporting it with examples and details to convince your readers of your point of view.

Clothes Tell Only Part

When I was living in Arizona, I went to a school that made students wear uniforms. I liked that idea, but when we moved to Illinois the school that I went to didn't have uniforms. I thought uniforms would be a good idea, so I talked with the principle.

Uniforms would be a good idea because people judge others too quickly. "Look at that shirt and pants, I bet she got that from k-mart, how ugly, I got this outfit from Ralph Luaren." With uniforms nobody will get judged or made fun of. That way the school will be more disciplined.

It's not only good for students and staff but good for parents too. Think of all the money you could save on detergent. There wouldn't be as many clothes to wash. For kids, if you're at recess or gym class and you were wearing your favorite pants that you got from Ralph Luaren or Tommy Hilphiger, you could easily fall and rip them.

Clothes help us show part of our personalities. But I think that what's inside matter most of all. My cousin is really into basketball so he always wears his bulls jersey

Continued on next page

> all the time. But when people look at him and they know
> he likes basketball, but you wouldn't know if he is a nice
> person or not.
>
> I know that clothes only tell part of how you really
> are inside. But what counts is the way you take attitude
> towards life.

Score 2

This essay about wearing uniforms has an effective opening and an appealing voice. However, the argument gets sidetracked into a discussion of what clothes tell about their wearers. Some sentences are awkward, wordy, and/or overconnected with conjunctions. Errors such as a run-on sentence in paragraph two, misspellings, lack of capitalization *(k-mart, bulls),* and an incorrect verb form *(what's inside matter most of all)* significantly detract from the piece.

PROMPT Write a persuasive essay for your classmates about something you would like to change at school. State your suggestion, supporting it with examples and details to convince your readers of your point of view.

No Homework

There shouldn't be no homework on the weekends. We need time to do what we want. Like hang out with our friends and a million other things. We have too much homework during the week. We shouldn't have homework during the weekend to make time for sports and relaxing. My cousin Ray he studies maybe six hours over the weekend which I think is ridiculous. Me and my friends prefer to just chill out.

We should have longer recess too. Recess is too short so we should have 2 instead of 1. And pizza every day for lunch. We should have a party on Fridays and watch DVDs. We're only kids once so give us a break.

Score 1

This essay is too disorganized and full of errors to be effective. The initial argument for having no weekend homework shifts to requests for longer recess, pizza for lunch, and Friday parties. Faulty conventions include a double negative *(shouldn't be no homework)*, sentence fragments, and pronoun errors *(My cousin Ray he; Me and my friends prefer to just chill out.).*

Write a research report about an aspect of an ancient culture or civilization. Write a clear thesis statement. Find information in sources such as books, magazines, CD-ROMs, and the Internet.

Ancient Romans: Great Architects

Ancient Roman architecture proves that ancient Rome was an advanced civilization. Study the remains of ancient Roman buildings. The materials and unique features of the buildings show that the ancient Romans were great architects.

Ancient Roman architects used materials they found in the earth for their buildings. Some of the oldest buildings were made with rock from volcanoes called tuff. A type of limestone was used to construct the Colosseum and other buildings. Ancient Romans also used marble, bronze, stucco, and their own form of concrete.

With these materials, ancient Romans constructed beautiful buildings with unique features. Columns, used to support a building, were not only strong but elegant. The arch was another feature of Roman architecture. Arches were used for bridges and aqueducts.

Some of the most famous buildings in the world were built by the ancient Romans. The Colosseum is a huge amphitheater that could hold 45,000 people. Part of the Colosseum is still standing. Another famous building is

Continued on next page

the Pantheon, a large domed structure with columns. The inside of the Pantheon contains spectacular marble and bronze decorations.

    Ancient Roman buildings reflect the people who built them. As Encyclopedia Britannica says, "Roman architecture was almost as complex as the Roman Empire itself." The remains of the buildings they constructed show the creativity and skill of the ancient Romans.

Score 4

This report is focused on the topic of ancient Roman architecture. It is organized logically with a thesis statement followed by paragraphs with strong topic sentences and good elaboration. Writing is formal, yet engaging. Writer shows knowledge of the subject. Specific words and a supporting quotation strengthen the report. Fluent sentences have varied lengths and structures. There is excellent control of grammar, capitalization, spelling, and punctuation.

PROMPT

Write a research report about an aspect of an ancient culture or civilization. Write a clear thesis statement. Find information in sources such as books, magazines, CD-ROMs, and the Internet.

Ancient Egyptian Women

The women of ancient Egypt had an unusual degree of freedom. Even by today's standards. Thousands of years ago, other cultures were shocked that Egyptian women could pursue activities such as trading goods at the market. The rights of ordinary women, the lives of religious women, and the reigns of women pharaohs show that ancient Egyptians were ahead of their time.

Ordinary Egyptian women shared many rights with Egyptian men. Women worked at jobs besides homemaking and earned the same wages as men. Some Egyptian women even worked in the military. Women of all classes could purchase land and decide what to do with it.

A common job for women was that of priestess. Priestesses led spiritual celebrations and mourned the dead, they had a voice in politics and a position of leadership in society.

Some women even became pharaohs. Pharaohs were rulers of ancient Egypt. Six women, begining with Neithikret around 2148 B.C. and ending with Cleopatra VII in 30 B.C., reigned as pharaoh. They led the military, financial, and social activities of ancient Egypt.

Continued on next page

> Ancient Egyptian women enjoyed rights that women in other cultures have won only recently. In fact, many women are currently struggling to achieve the legal and financial equality that ancient Egyptian women had.

Score 3

This research report is organized logically with a strong thesis statement followed by paragraphs with clear topic sentences. The tone is matter-of-fact, yet personable. Writer shows knowledge of the subject. Word choice is effective, and sentences are varied. A misspelling *(begining)*, a fragment, and a run-on prevent the report from getting a top score.

Write a research report about an aspect of an ancient culture or civilization. Write a clear thesis statement. Find information in sources such as books, magazines, CD-ROMs, and the Internet.

The Mayan Civilization

The Mayan civilization is so cool. The Maya were really American Indian people. Everybody in the family like the parents, children, and grandparents all lived together. They built big temples. They raised turkeys and honeybees on there farms.

I'm from Guatemala, and I think I'm really lucky to be born in a country that have one of the oldest civilizations in the world.

Tikal is one of the cities that have temples there. Tikal is a city in the Northern part of Guatemala. In Tikal, there is a lot of trees, so animals like monkeys and birds like all around there. Sometimes you can hear the animals yelling. Tikal is also the biggest and most ancient ruin of Mayan civilization that anyone had ever excavated. Just the city alone had forty-thousand Mayan Indians living there!

The Mayan Indians loved art. They made a lot of pottery and statues. Some of the statues that archeoligists found were statues of possibly Indians. No one really knows how they looked, so a lot of people think they looked like the statues.

Continued on next page

> The Mayan temples are really big. They stand 20,000 feet off the ground. When you visit the temples and climb to the top, all you see is an ocean of green trees. It's amazing. Mabey someday you should visit the Mayan temples!

Score 2

Information provided is generally interesting, although the thesis statement is weak. Voice is warm and enthusiastic, but often too informal for this type of report. Wording is sometimes awkward or repetitive *(a lot of)*. Conventions errors include a lack of agreement between subject and verb *(country that have one of the oldest civilizations; there is a lot of trees)* and misspellings.

Write a research report about an aspect of an ancient culture or civilization. Write a clear thesis statement. Find information in sources such as books, magazines, CD-ROMs, and the Internet.

Ancient Greeks and Their Gods

The Ancient Greeks, like many other cultures, would make up stories to help explain things in nature. For instance some stories would tell why there are echoes or why there are spiders. Although the majority of Greek tales were for pleasure, many stories do explain things that we even see being done today.

One of the stories of the Greeks is about a nymph named Echo. She was the best liked of all of the nymphs. Although she was pretty and kind she was known for her beautiful voice. The goddess of love, Aphrodite, would come from Olympus to talk to Echo. One day Aphrodite asked Echo if she wished for anyone to love her. If so she would send her son Eros (Cupid) to hit him with a magic arrow so he would fall madly in love with Echo. Echo replied no, she didn't see a man who pleased her yet. So Echo bid farewell to Aphrodite and went into the forest. There she saw the mighty god Zeus flirting with another nymph. She also saw Zeus's wife, Hera, walking toward him. So Echo ran in front of Hera and told her that a couple of minutes ago Zeus came to this same wood looking for Hera. Surprised Hera went to

Continued on next page

Olympus looking for her husband. In the mean time Zeus heard their voices and hid in some bushes. After his wife left he came out and to thank Echo and gave her a ring. After discovering that Zeus was not at Olympus she angrily went back to the forest to scold Echo. She saw Echo admiring a ring on her finger and recognized the ring as her husbands. After realizing that she had been tricked Hera put a curse on Echo. Since Echo used her voice for lying she couldn't say anything except the last words said to her. After the curse was made, Hera left the crying nymph to go look for her husband. While running back to her home Echo met a boy about her own age. She fell in love with him at first sight. However the boy ignored her after he found out that she would only repeat what he said. Once again Echo was left crying alone in the forest. After the boy left Echo felt such sadness that she started to pray to Aphrodite. She asked Aphrodite to make her dissappear. Aphrodite obeyed the request and Echo disappeared though her voice stayed because Aphrodite could not bear to lose her voice. Echo did not ask revenge on the boy for leaving her, but Aphrodite still punished the boy. She

Continued on next page

would make him fall in love with someone who could not return his love. But the boy unknowing of his curse sat down by a river to rest. He then looked into the water and saw a face. It was the most beautiful face he had ever seen. He fell in love with it at first sight. However whenever he tried to touch the face it disappeared. So he sat by the river staring at the face until he grew into the flower Narcissus. And you can still find the flower Narcissus on the riverbank. You can also sometimes find Echo in the woods.

    This Ancient Greek story above tells why there is Narcissus along riverbanks and echoes in the forest. Other stories tell why there is fire or all of the ill things in the world like spiders. These stories were important to many people long ago and are still enjoyed today.

Score 1

The response does not address the prompt. The final paragraph attempts, but fails, to provide a rationale for labeling the retelling of a myth as a research paper. Parts of the plot are confusing, and many sentences are wordy. The voice is flat and somewhat disengaged. Errors in conventions include misspellings, lack of paragraphing and punctuation, unclear pronoun referents, and omission of commas after introductory clauses in complex sentences.